The Technological Entrepreneur's Playbook

The Technological Entrepreneur's Playbook

Ian Chaston

BEP BUSINESS EXPERT PRESS

The Technological Entrepreneur's Playbook

First published in 2017 by
Business Expert Press, LLC
222 East 46th Street, New York, NY 10017
www.businessexpertpress.com

ISBN-13: 978-1-63157-840-3 (paperback)
ISBN-13: 978-1-63157-841-0 (e-book)

Business Expert Press Entrepreneurship and Small Business Management Collection

Collection ISSN: 1946-5653 (print)
Collection ISSN: 1946-5661 (electronic)

Cover and interior design by Exeter Premedia Services Private Ltd., Chennai, India

First edition: 2017

10 9 8 7 6 5 4 3 2 1

Printed in the United States of America.

Abstract

As exemplified by Apple and Google, maximizing the wealth of organizations involves what Joseph Schumpeter described as "creative destruction." This occurs when scientific or technological breakthroughs lead to the launch of a radically new product or service at a time when there often is little or no evidence of the existence of an identified market opportunity. The world is currently involved in the third Industrial Revolution and academic research and real-world case studies have validated the fact that the management of technology-driven entrepreneurship is a somewhat different process to that of market-driven entrepreneurship. The existence of these differences generates the perspective that benefit exists in identifying managerial guidelines that can be of assistance in ensuring the success of technological entrepreneurship projects in both start-ups and existing businesses. Hence the aim of this text is to draw upon academic theory and real-world case materials as the basis for defining 86 key managerial guidelines for optimizing the outcome from involvement in technological entrepreneurship.

Keywords

business start-ups, disruption, entrepreneurship, managerial guidelines, market-driven entrepreneurship, radical innovation, technological entrepreneurship, technology-based innovation, wealth generation

Contents

Preface

The aim of this text is to draw upon academic theory and real-world case materials as the basis for defining key guidelines necessary to optimize the outcomes from involvement in technological entrepreneurship.

Most texts, university courses, and corporate training programs have the start point in the entrepreneurial process as the identification of new market opportunities, thereby providing the basis for the development of a radically new product or service proposition. Given the high number of commercial successes achieved by this market-driven approach, this clearly is a valid and viable way of creating new firms and sustaining the performance of existing organizations.

Nevertheless, it is important to register that in terms of maximizing the wealth of organizations and even entire nations, the most economically impactful entrepreneurial outcomes are the result of what Joseph Schumpeter, the father of modern entrepreneurship theory, described as "creative destruction" leading to the decline, and sometimes, the total disappearance of existing industrial sectors. Schumpeter opined that the most successful form of innovation is technology-driven. This occurs with scientific or technological breakthroughs and experimentation leading to the launch of a radically new product or service at a time when there often is little evidence of the existence of an identified market opportunity. Subsequent to the emergence of Schumpeter's theories, both academic research and real-world case studies have validated the fact that the management of technology-driven entrepreneurship is a somewhat different process to that of market-driven entrepreneurship. As demonstrated by firms such of Apple and Google, the existence of this difference generates the perspective that benefit exists in identifying the managerial guidelines that can be of assistance in ensuring the success of technological entrepreneurship projects in both start-ups and existing businesses.

The guidelines presented in Chapter 1 are generated by a review of economic trends, understanding the nature of entrepreneurship, and the differences that exist between technology-driven versus market-driven entrepreneurial activity. Chapter 2 presents the guidelines associated with understanding the traits and behaviors of the technological entrepreneur. This is followed in Chapter 3 by coverage of issues associated with the creation and management of entrepreneurial enterprises.

Opportunity recognition is a critical aspect of successful entrepreneurship. The nature of this process in relation to the guidelines for effective idea generation and subsequent development activities of the technological entrepreneur are examined in Chapter 4.

The source of entrepreneurial opportunities is not restricted to events within core market systems, but can also emerge as the result of changes in the macroenvironment. Hence, Chapter 5 presents the guidelines concerning how by understanding these latter sources of change, this can lead to the identification of new entrepreneurial opportunities.

Opportunity exploitation cannot succeed unless the individual and/or organization has the appropriate competences. Chapter 6 examines the nature of the competences required in order to successfully engage in technological entrepreneurship. The initial launch of entrepreneurial products or services usually occurs based on an intuitive rather than a logic-based strategic philosophy. The ways in which emergent strategies can be created, developed, and evolved over time as a result of market experience are covered in Chapter 7. The management of technological entrepreneurship involves some unique organizational processes. These are covered in Chapter 8. Success in radical innovation is usually critically dependent on the acquisition and exploitation of new knowledge. Chapter 9 reviews the necessary guidelines for exploiting new knowledge within the entrepreneurship process.

A characteristic of many developed nation economies is that the service sector now provides the majority of these countries' GDP. Chapter 10 reviews the guidelines associated with the exploitation of technological entrepreneurship to enhance the growth and expansion of service sector organizations. Another characteristic of developed economies is the exponential rise in the cost of health care reflecting the influence of advances in medical treatment and the demand pressures caused by population aging. Vital for the ongoing success of any economy are the ways can be found to stabilize or even reduce health care costs. Chapter 11 examines the opportunities associated with the exploitation of technological entrepreneurship within the health care sector. Chapter 12 is the final chapter in which some of the current advances in science and technology offer new opportunities for future entrepreneurial outcomes.

One target readership group is undergraduates and postgraduates, especially in the science and technology disciplines, who are taking courses in subjects such as innovation, small business management, or business strategy. The other target audience is individuals who are team members, or individuals who are managing teams, engaged in scientific or technological innovation.

CHAPTER 1

Technology: The Wealth Generator

The Wealth of Nations

For thousands of years, wealth generation was based on trade or invading other countries and repatriating their wealth. This economic model was changed forever during the first Industrial Revolution. This occurred because technological entrepreneurs demonstrated that the creation of new forms of motive power and the development of new machines could move a nation from an agriculture-based economy to one centered around factory-based, large-scale manufacturing.

Industrialization cannot prevent the occurrence of economic cycles with periods of rising prosperity followed by economic downturns and rising unemployment. Factors that influence these cycles are (a) the belief that ownership of a specific asset would always lead to ever-increasing wealth, (b) the assumption that future income or gain in the value of assets would permit debt repayment, and (c) imbalances emerging between supply and demand. Evidence of the ongoing truism of economic cycles has recently been illustrated following the onset of the global downturn that commenced in 2007, from which many countries have yet to recover.

The catalyst for the weakened state of the global economy was the subprime mortgage fiasco in the United States where financial institutions approved loans to individuals who lacked the income sufficient to service the debt they had been persuaded to assume. As the scale of the problem became apparent, financial institutions either failed or had to be rescued by government intervention. Similar problems also emerged in Ireland and United Kingdom. These events were followed by recognition that in some countries in Europe, such as Greece and Spain, the level of public sector expenditure had become unsustainable. The outcome was the sovereign debt crisis that has been a massive burden dragging down the entire European Union (EU).

Meanwhile, multinational companies in sectors such as coal, oil, and minerals continued to invest in capacity expansion on the false premise of continued rising growth in the Chinese economy. When the first signs of a slowdown emerged in the Chinese economy, a massive decline in commodity prices was triggered. This had a devastating impact, especially in those countries reliant upon commodity exports as their primary source of economic growth and stability.

Even Milk Can Be Risky

White Gold

Case Aims: To illustrate the risks associated with an over reliance upon agriculture

New Zealand's economy has been highly reliant upon agricultural output. Since World War II, dairy farming has become the dominant agricultural sector. A key problem is the country's remote location relative to overseas markets, and milk is a highly perishable product. This situation led to the creation of Fonterra that was granted a near monopoly over the purchase of milk and assigned the task of using milk as a raw material to move the country further up the food industry value chain (Baldwin 2015).

Although raw milk production in New Zealand has risen dramatically, Fonterra's success in moving into branded goods has been limited. As a consequence, the strategy of the company has been to invest in expanding the capability of converting raw milk into milk powder. This is essentially a commodity product, and hence, profit margins have remained relatively low.

New Zealand's reputation for high quality has proved important in exploiting the growing demand for milk powder in China. As the Chinese economy continued to expand, New Zealand enjoyed a period of unprecedented economic growth. Furthermore, the country's conservative banking sector practices and public sector spending meant the country was not adversely impacted by the Great Recession caused by the subprime mortgage in the United States and the sovereign debt crisis in Europe. As a consequence, by 2013, New Zealand's self-perception was of a country enjoying a "golden age" of wealth generation.

Fonterra's success relied upon rising market demand and minimal milk powder capacity expansion elsewhere in the world. In recent years, other countries have expanded milk powder production capacity in seeking to obtain a foothold in Asian markets. Further price competition emerged when the EU banned exports to Russia in response to the crisis in the Ukraine, causing more European producers to increase their efforts to develop new markets in the Far East. In 2014, the world milk powder market followed the pattern of other commodity markets of moving from boom to bust. The weakening Chinese economy and competition from elsewhere in the world resulted in a collapse in milk powder demand, with the resultant requirement of Fonterra needing to slash farm-gate milk prices. With dairy products representing almost 25 percent of the total exports and milk prices lower than the cost of production, recognition of the adverse impact of these events was reflected in growing concerns about the debt levels within the farming industry (Gray 2016).

Playbook Guideline 1: Avoid excessive reliance on commodities on the hopes that this offers a source of secure long-term wealth generation

The Importance of Innovation

Organizations that have enjoyed an extended period of profitability tend to become complacent about the future, and over time, operating costs tend to rise. New competitors, often based overseas, are not only assisted by rising costs within the incumbent firms, but are also often able to exploit advantages, such as lower labor or raw materials costs, thereby permitting them to compete on the basis of much lower prices (Nuvolari and Verspagen 2009).

Alert organizations are aware that standing still is a guarantee for moving backward. To avoid this outcome, these organizations have to accept the importance of sustaining investment in innovation. It can be considered that there are three dimensions to innovation. These are (1) product versus process, (2) radical versus incremental, and (3) competence enhancement. Product innovation results in an improved or new product or service proposition. Process innovation activity results in improving the effectiveness and efficiencies of production (Datta, Mukherjee, and Jessup 2015).

A long-established management philosophy is that, higher revenue comes from maximizing the retention time for products or services within the maturity phase of the product life cycle (or PLC). The means many firms focus on incremental innovation involving the launch of new, improved version of an existing product or service. An attraction of incremental innovation is that the investment costs are usually relatively small and the risk of market failure extremely low.

Another source of innovation is sectoral architecture, which is concerned with the relationships and interactions that a firm has created within a supply chain. A new firm may encounter obstacles in becoming accepted as a member of an existing sectoral architecture. One way of overcoming this problem is by creating a new, radically innovative alternative architecture. Such was the case with Michael Dell. At a time when other personal computer (PC) manufacturers were using either a sales force or a network of distributors to generate sales, he entered the market by using direct marketing and mail order to service customer needs. Over time, Dell has continually sought to add competitive advantage by further developing architectural innovation and has created a distinctive global, virtual supply network (Lawton and Michaels 2001).

Playbook Guideline 2: Risk minimization and minimal investment in innovation generates minimal financial returns

Detergents Facing an Emerging Risk?

Case Aims: To illustrate that even in low-tech sectors, the unexpected may occur

In a world increasingly concerned with adopting a more sustainable orientation toward the consumption of energy and natural resources, an obvious target for change is the humble washing machine. Interest in how to reduce water and energy consumption led researchers at Leeds University to examine the potential of using a large number of small nylon beads to fulfill the cleaning action within a washing machine.

The researchers discovered that by adding only a small amount of water sufficient to dissolve the stains on clothes and temporarily alter the molecular structure of the polymer beads, which gently rub against the materials being washed, it was possible to reduce water usage by 70 percent. Furthermore, the reduced water usage means that compared to conventional machines, as there is no longer a need for a rinse or spin cycle, energy consumption can be reduced by up to 98 percent, and carbon dioxide (CO_2) emissions reduced by approximately 40 percent. This breakthrough, which may become a problem for manufacturers of conventional washing machines, may possibly have even greater significant long-term adverse implications for the multinationals that currently dominate the global market for detergents.

To exploit the new approach to laundering clothes, spin-off company named Xeros Ltd has been created to market the technology (www.xeroscleaning.com). Led by CEO Mark Nichols, the company is seeking to refine every aspect of their polymer bead cleaning system in areas such enhancing bead absorbency and upgrading the efficiency of washing machines that utilize the new technology. To assist ongoing developments, the firm has entered into a partnership with BASF, the world's largest chemical company, to investigate alternative bead chemistries for use in washing machines and custom-tailored detergents.

Playbook Guideline 3: Avoid complacency because in the end, everything has the potential to be impacted by unforeseen changes

Innovation

Radical innovation generates entirely different new products, services, processes, or delivery systems. As demonstrated by firms such as Apple and Google, the reward is exceptionally high profitability. Radicalness is a function of uniqueness when compared with currently available market offerings or production processes. The most radical innovations are new to the world and differ massively from existing products, services, or processes. In contrast, incremental innovation involves adaptations and refinements to existing products, services, processes, or delivery systems (Burgelman and McKinney 2006). Once an organization has successfully launched a radical innovation, this same organization will usually seek to sustain market dominance by also engaging in incremental innovations. An example is provided by Microsoft, which having radically altered the approach to the provision of computer software for PCs, has subsequently sought to retain market leadership through successive releases of the new Windows operating systems and the firm's suite of Office software products.

Playbook Guideline 4: High-risk radical innovation offers the reward of much greater financial return

Retaining Leadership in the Innovation Stakes

Case Aims: To illustrate that technological innovation demands a long-term commitment to retaining market leadership through superior capability

In the 1920s, Henry Ford revolutionized the car industry by introducing production processes, which he observed in Chicago meat packing plants. His new approach was so successful that a new, rapidly accepted industry convention was established; namely to be successful, a high-volume car manufacturer must be capable of utilizing mass production manufacturing to supply customers with a low-cost, standard product.

Although before World War II some car manufacturers engaged in innovation, this tended to be of an incremental nature, leading to product improvements such as automatic gearboxes, power steering, and hydraulic brakes. Following the end of World War II, price continued to be the critical factor influencing the purchase decision of the average customer. This had the implication that successful firms needed to maximize manufacturing productivity. Less effort was allocated to involvement in innovation. Instead, the primary focus was that of achieving economies of scale. This was usually delivered through industrial mergers between domestic producers, eventually leading to only one or two firms dominating each Western World home markets (e.g., Ford, General Motors in the United States; British Leyland, subsequently Rover Group, in the UK, Volkswagen in Germany; Fiat in Italy, Renault; and Citroen in France) (Helper and Henderson 2014).

The OPEC oil crisis in the 1970s sparked higher customer interest in fuel economy, offering both European and Japanese producers the opportunity to break into the largest car market in the world, the United States. While the U.S. car makers were struggling with the problems of learning how to make smaller cars and manage in what had become a highly unionized production environment, the Japanese were left to experiment with concepts such as robotics, just in time (JIT) to further enhance productivity and total quality management (TQM) to improve "'build quality." Their success permitted them to become global players in the world car market. Many of the Japanese's advances in manufacturing, which took firms such as Toyota and Honda to market leadership, were often achieved by being willing to challenge industrial conventions established by the major Western manufacturers (Townsend and Calantone 2014).

Long lead times can exist between concept identification, completion of fundamental research, and the ability to launch a new product based on a new technology. An example of being prepared to invest in the acquisition of new knowledge and internal capabilities is provided by Toyota. Long before the American or European car manufacturers exhibited any concerns over rising oil prices, Toyota, as the world's leading automobile manufacturer, had the strategic insight to research how to move vehicle transportation away from a dependence on hydrocarbons to utilize other types of fuels. Their first product was the highly successful hybrid the Toyota Prius. Having launched the Prius, the company has focused on continuous innovation to improve this vehicle and to expand the company's hybrid product line (Rapp 2007).

The expected next alternative to cars using petrol is the fuel–cell vehicle, or FCV. These vehicles run on electricity generated by combining hydrogen with oxygen, with only water vapor being the byproduct. Two major constraints, similar to the initial hurdle facing electric cars, are the high development costs and the lack of refuelling infrastructure. Toyota's solution has been to offer its fuel cell components and FCV patents and patents for the installation and operation of hydrogen fuelling stations to others companies free of charge until 2020. Although the move risks Toyota compromising its technological leadership in the FCV technology, the decision is perceived as less important than the need to stimulate an industry-wide effort to rapidly expand the infrastructure required to achieve rapid market penetration for the new technology. Toyota's decision comes ahead of the launch of its new fuel–cell sedan, the hydrogen-powered Mirai, in the United States and Europe in 2015 (Muller 2015).

Playbook Guideline 5: Staying ahead requires an ongoing commitment to engaging in radical and incremental innovation

Entrepreneurship

French economist Jean-Baptiste Say is credited with inventing the term "entrepreneurship" in the early 19th century. At the time, the concept was not seen as important by mainstream economists (Dorobaț 2014). It would not be until the 1920s that the Austrian economist Joseph Schumpeter challenged the classic economic theory and proposed an alternative paradigm for explaining fundamental economic change. Schumpeter (1934) noted that profits decline when technologies mature and the emergence of new technologies permit new winners to emerge. He described this process as "creative destruction," in which entrepreneurs exploit a new technology as the basis for the creation of entirely new industries, while concurrently existing, mature industries become increasingly unable to sustain wealth generation.

Schumpeter's primary focus was on entrepreneurship in which a new technology, often during an economically turbulent period, provides the basis for new businesses, and that as a result of creative destruction, this become a nation's new primary source of wealth generation. Subsequently, Schumpeter (1954) concluded that existing larger firms are less likely to engage in creative destruction. Instead, they tended to engage in "creative accumulation" by exploiting their accumulated knowledge in the development of the next generation of products and services. This scenario can be contrasted with creative destruction, which involves a widening of innovation by new firms entering the market and successfully challenging incumbents by exploiting new forms of technology.

Playbook Guideline 6: Creative destruction permits the development of new to the world products and the creation of new sectors of industry

Israel Kirzner (1973) rejected Schumpeter's perspective that entrepreneurs develop new propositions without initial reference or influence of market forces. Kirzner's viewpoint was that entrepreneurs are engaged in moving resources from areas of low productivity to a different area where profitability had the potential to be much higher. The catalyst for action is the entrepreneur being alert to new market opportunities that can be exploited through some form of innovation. This is in contrast to Schumpeter perspective. He did not see entrepreneurship as a demand-driven process, but rather it is entrepreneurship that forces changes in output and consumer tastes.

Available evidence seems to indicate that both Schumpeter and Kirzner's perspectives are equally valid. This perspective can be seen in the distinction made between technology-driven versus market-driven entrepreneurship (Habtay 2012). Technology-push entrepreneurship occurs where scientific breakthroughs and R&D experimentation precede market opportunity analysis and the development of a viable business proposition. In contrast, market-driven entrepreneurship begins with the customers creating demand pressure, thereby permitting identification of new market opportunities that provide the basis of innovation that precedes a firm's investment in product or service development activities. This latter form of entrepreneurial change typically emerges when a market often originally created as the result of disruptive technological entrepreneurship has matured and market-driven entrepreneurship based around a revised business model becomes a more likely strategy for sustaining ongoing success.

Habtay proposed that the start point for market-driven entrepreneurship is the discovery of viable new customer value propositions and the identification of a viable customer segment. The other dimension is a market structure that permits the creation of a business model that permits the focal firm to effectively exploit the identified market opportunity. As illustrated in Figure 1.1, in the case of technology-driven entrepreneurship, it is new scientific or technological knowledge that results in a push for development, eventually leading a commercially viable outcome. Market-opportunity entrepreneurship can be considered as a pull-directed process because recognition of potential customer need is the catalyst that prompts the development activity. It should be recognized, however, that in responding to market pull, exploitation of new scientific or technological knowledge may be required to create a viable commercial solution.

In considering which of the two options, market-driven or technology-driven entrepreneurship, offers the greatest source of long-term wealth generation, both history and the current day evidence clearly indicate the superiority of the latter philosophy. The first Industrial Revolution generated huge wealth for the UK entrepreneurs involved. Similarly, the second Industrial Revolution, which centered around the exploitation of electricity and the internal combustion engine, made individuals such as

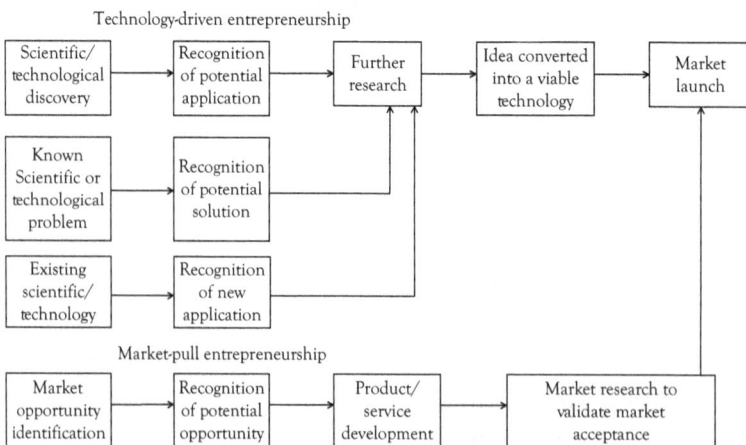

Figure 1.1 A comparison of entrepreneurial processes

Thomas Edison extremely rich. Today, during the third Industrial Revolution, which is focused on exploiting the Internet and related technologies, the world's two most valuable companies, in terms of their traded share values, are Apple and Google.

Playbook Guideline 7: Individuals and organizations seeking to maximize long-term wealth should focus on exploiting technology-driven entrepreneurship

Technology-Based Destruction

Case Aims: To illustrate the technological opportunities offered by Internet-based has created a new "sharing economy," which can adversely impact existing, long-established service businesses

Advances in computing, the Internet, and the emergence of new technologies, such as the smartphone, can be considered as providing the basis for the latest Industrial Revolution. This situation has led to the emergence of new forms of creative destruction. One form of creative destruction is being achieved by new companies engaged in what has become known as the "sharing economy." This involves new companies, such as the taxi firm Uber, developing new ways to exploit the Internet and associated emerging technologies to support web platforms that bring together individuals who have underutilized assets with people who would like to rent those assets over the short term (Cusumano 2015).

Uber started life in San Francisco as a private limousine service. In 2010, the company launched a smartphone app that enabled potential customers to call for a ride, get a price quote, and then accept or reject it. The providers of the ride are independent drivers who pay Uber a commission for being linked to customers. The regulations that apply to conventional taxi companies do not usually apply to Uber drivers, and hence, these individuals can provide customers with lower-cost rides in smaller, less expensive cars. To expand their fleet of drivers, Uber helps individual drivers get loans to buy new cars, which permits them to deliver the service. Not required to meet certain regulations for in relation to the provision of transportation services, such as insurance, training of drivers, and licenses means, Uber can outcompete the existing taxi firms. Uber drivers can also decline to provide service when they do not like the requested destination. This is a behavior that existing taxi companies cannot exploit because they are obligated to offer standardized prices and provide service to anyone who calls.

Another example of the sharing economy is provided by Airbnb. This started in 2007 in San Francisco when the founders had extra rooms to rent and decided to offer a low-cost air mattress and bed and breakfast to attendees at a local conference. They created a website to target cities with conferences and signed up people with spare rooms. Subsequently, the company has expanded by offering the service to anybody looking for low-cost accommodation. By September 2014, Airbnb had expanded to 800,000 room listings in 190 countries and claims to have attracted 17 million customers (Helm 2014). Not surprisingly, within the hotel industry, the unions have reacted strongly to this threat by demanding city regulators take action over what may be breaches of regulations regarding private hosting and subletting (Fox 2016). There is also the potential for a major loss in tax revenues in those cities where there are a large number of hotels generating high-level valued-added taxes.

Playbook Guideline 8: Focus on exploiting new or emerging technologies when seeking to radically change long-established industries

Definitions

The Oxford English dictionary defines the entrepreneurship as the activity of an individual who "attempt to profit by risk and initiative." This is a somewhat broad perspective that many people would probably consider could be associated with broad range of activities, only some of which can be perceived as entrepreneurial. In an attempt to propose a definition that could provide a framework for determining whether an individual or an organization can be considered as being entrepreneurial, Chaston (2016) posited that the outcome of all innovation is some form of change. In the majority of situations, innovation achieves an incremental improvement in a product, service, or process. The magnitude of change does not require any significant behavior shift by customers in order to be able to utilize the innovation. Examples of conventional innovation in the world of branded goods include a detergent that has better whitening power or the addition of new flavors to expand the variety of canned soups that are made available to consumers.

This situation can be contrasted with entrepreneurial innovation where there is a fundamental change in an existing product, service, or process or the introduction of a totally new to the world proposition. In such cases, utilization of the new offering will involve significant education of the potential user to make available new understanding that is necessary to gain widespread market adoption. Even more importantly, entrepreneurial innovation will usually have the potential to replace these existing propositions, in some cases on a scale that renders these latter goods completely obsolete. On the basis of this outcome, Chaston proposed the following definition, namely:

> *Entrepreneurship is an activity which disrupts existing market conventions and/or leads to the emergence of totally new conventions.*

In terms of this current text, the preceding definition provides the following basis for defining the role of technology-driven change, namely:

> *Technological entrepreneurship is an activity involving the exploitation of a new, emerging or existing technology which disrupt existing market conventions and/or leads to the creation of totally new conventions.*

Technological Convention Disruption

Case Aims: To illustrate how an entrepreneurial idea can emerge and evolve over time as the founders gain understanding of the potential for market disruption

At the beginning of the saga that led to the creation of the first Apple computer, Steve Jobs' primary interest was to eventually start a business. It was his close friend Steve Wozniak who first had the idea of creating a PC. He had already designed a terminal with a keyboard and monitor that could be connected to a minicomputer. His vision was to locate the microprocessor inside the terminal and the idea for a stand-alone computer of PC was created. Having assembled his creation, he developed the code necessary to permit the use of the keyboard to display letters on the computer screen (Isaacson 2011).

At this juncture, Steve Jobs proposed Wozniak's idea could be used to make money by building and selling the printed circuit boards that could carry a microprocessor, offering eight kilobytes of memory that could be programmed using BASIC. Their first potential customer was Paul Terrell who owned a computer store, the Byte Shop. He was not impressed with the circuit board idea and insisted he be supplied with assembled boards on which the microprocessor was already installed. When Jobs delivered the boards, it became apparent that Terrell had expected a more complete product that included a power supply, case, monitor, and keyboard. Jobs accepted the validity of Terrell's perspective, which acted as the catalyst for the vision of PCs needing to come in a complete package based on the hardware being encased, the keyboard being built-in, provision of a power supply, and the inclusion of appropriate software. The outcome was the world famous PC icon, the Apple computer. This product successfully challenged and disrupted existing conventions within the computer industry, eventually providing the basis for a new worldwide global product convention.

Playbook Guideline 9: Technological entrepreneurship can create an entirely new-to-the-world proposition or radically change an existing sector of industry

Entrepreneurial Infrastructure

There is a romantic appeal about single entrepreneur or a small group of entrepreneurs laboring away in a garage or university laboratory, which results in a completely new technological innovation and the subsequent launch of a world-beating product or service proposition. Although such events will continue to occur, the frequency can be expected to remain somewhat low. This is because as technology becomes more complex, it is increasingly difficult for an individual or small group of individuals to have the knowledge and resources that are demanded during the development and commercialization of radically new, technology-based propositions. These interactions can be considered as components within a technological ecosystem of the type summarized in Figure 1.2.

The importance of Silicon Valley, California, as a the leading source of entrepreneurial wealth generation is illustrated by the fact that in 2010, the ZIP code 95054 in Silicon Valley produced more industrial patents than any other ZIP code in the United States. Engel and del-Palacio (2011) posited this scale of success of firms can be attributed to the area being the world's leading "Cluster of Innovation." The cluster's ecosystem is composed of start-ups, professional service firms that support the start-up process, and mature enterprises that remain focused on sustaining long-term growth through ongoing emphasis on technology-based entrepreneurship.

Engel and del-Palacio (2015) posited that Silicon Valley, along with other Centers of Innovation elsewhere in the world key are critically reliant on entrepreneurs being supported by an infrastructure constituted of venture capital investors, mature corporations acting as strategic

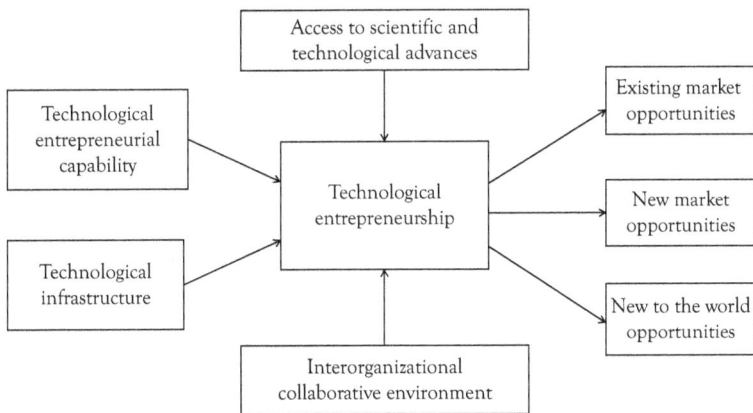

Figure 1.2 Inputs and outputs within the technological entrepreneurship ecosystem

investors, universities, government, R&D centers, and specialized service providers. Developing and exploiting new technology usually demands massive expenditure. In the case of start-ups, a critically important aspect of Silicon Valley infrastructure is the presence of venture capitalists that have both the expertise and "deep pockets" to fund the activities of new, emergent entrepreneurial firms.

Engel and del-Palacio noted that the large companies in the area recognize the importance of investing in new technology, either internally or providing collaborative support for smaller firms. Engaging in this scale of expenditure is only made possible because large companies, such as Apple and Google, have accumulated huge cash reserves that can be made available to fund the commercialization of new technologies. Other infrastructure components that Engel and del-Palacio consider important within a cluster of innovation is the presence of leading, research-orientated universities and research centers funded by governments to engage in blue sky and leading-edge research programs.

Playbook Guideline 10: Technological entrepreneurs can greatly enhance their potential for success by locating within an appropriate cluster of innovation

CHAPTER 2

Technological Entrepreneurs

Character Traits

Academics have sought to identify common traits that influence entrepreneurial behavior and attempt to link these traits to successful business outcomes (Steers, Sanchez-Runde, and Nardon 2012). Success in this area of endeavor has been limited. There are probably a number of reasons for this outcome. First, character traits found to be significant in relation to entrepreneurs are often similar to those found among other successful people such as politicians and outstanding sports people (Chell, Haworthy, and Brearley 1991). Second, there are a number of methodological problems measuring traits, including the fact that traits may change over time. Third, entrepreneurial success is usually because of the influence of a mix of variables such as the emergence of a viable technology, access to resources, and prevailing market demand.

Playbook Guideline 11: Do not attempt to categorize people, because technological entrepreneurs come in all different shapes and size

Vision

Vision can be considered as an overarching sense of purpose that drives current and future endeavors. In "how-to-do" manuals and academic texts, some authors insist that vision is a mandatory requirement from day one in order to ensure success. This perspective is supported by the evidence of the activities of some start-up businesses (Ashcroft, Holden, and Low 2009). From the outset, for example, Anita Roddick, the founder of *The Body Shop*, had the vision of wanting to create skin-care products made from natural ingredients and to avoid testing new products on animals, which was common practice among large manufacturers (Entine 1995).

Witt (1998) opined the technological entrepreneur often has no well-defined vision at the outset, but instead is single-mindedly committed to solving a scientific or technological problem. Only once they have solved the identified problem is much thought given to using the solution as the basis for a commercial venture. Only at this latter juncture does an "emergent market vision" develop. Furthermore, this vision often requires revision over time as the entrepreneur gains further understanding of what is involved in the creation and operation of a successful business.

Witt posited that a conception of a new business consists of subjective, sometimes idiosyncratic imaginings in the mind of the potential entrepreneur of what entity is to be created and how it is to be structured. This is because the business conception will be based on the entrepreneur's interpretation of information in relation to the relevance and meaning for their imagined business venture. Conversion of the business conception into an explicit framework tends to occur when the entrepreneur is required to communicate their vision to others such as potential customers and investors. This is because the vision provides a framework that permits them to understand the purpose of the new business idea. Once the new business is created, the vision can be important to the employees. Where the entrepreneurial business is not understood by the employees, it is difficult for the entrepreneur to create and sustain employee enthusiasm and motivation.

Playbook Guideline 12: Do not worry about vision, this often only emerges at a later date as understanding of the preferred technical solution emerges

Evolving a Personal Vision into an Entrepreneurial Proposition

Case Aims: To illustrate how an individual's vision may provide the basis for a viable, technology-driven entrepreneurial business

Anderson (1992) was deeply affected by the death of her father due the fact that in the 1950s, medical technology had been unable to diagnose his worsening heart condition. The outcome was a career in medical technology to find new ways of improving diagnostic techniques. One day, she was contacted by Dr. Stephen Boros at St. Paul Children's Hospital, who was treating baby boy born with a rare disorder that caused the child to stop breathing whenever he fell asleep. Carbon dioxide, or CO_2, in the blood controls the depth and frequency of breathing. To get the breathing rate just right, Boros sought a way of noninvasively measuring the baby's oxygen and CO_2.

Anderson, working on her kitchen table, developed a machine that permitted noninvasive measurements. This success prompted Anderson to convert her personal ideas into an entrepreneurial vision of creating a new business manufacturing machines and creating software that could enhance the medical profession's ability to diagnose heart and lung disease. The new company was known as Medical Graphics. Anderson's initial activities, as in most start-ups, were to make herself responsible for everything. Within a few years, Medical Graphics achieved over $3 million in sales by supplying a range of unique, noninvasive diagnostic solutions to the health care industry. With the aim of accelerating growth, the company diversified into nonmedical markets and expanded overseas. Eventually, the stress of running the business became excessive and Anderson stood down as the chief executive officer (CEO).

The board brought in experienced "professional managers." These individuals focused on the conventional approach of improving the bottom line and formalizing internal operational systems. During visits to the company, Anderson noticed a decline in motivation and enthusiasm, especially among the key research staff, and realized the conventional approach to managing had been accompanied by a loss of her original entrepreneurial vision.

Anderson decided to return. To reawaken understanding of her vision and to reinstill a common purpose, she focused on communicating to everybody that the primary role of the company was to prevent heart and lung disease, the leading causes of death and rising health care costs. To reinforce this message, she withdraw the company from all markets not directly related to this area of health care provision and put new innovative product development as the company's most important task.

Playbook Guideline 13: Never let the bean counters take over and destroy the technological entrepreneurial vision

Opportunity Orientation

The majority of new products or services are the consequence of the acquisition of market information, which identifies customer dissatisfaction or an unfulfilled need. Large organizations, especially in branded consumer goods markets, rely heavily on market research to assess consumer awareness, attitudes, and usage patterns. The advent of Big Data has provided firms with the ability to access and analyze much larger datasets by linking formal market research with real-time data from sources such as their own websites and social media. The potential drawback of relying on market data to identify new opportunities is when the customer is not able to articulate a specific future need (Key and Hufenbach 2014).

Technological entrepreneurs are less likely to be concerned with accessing market information at the outset of a new project. This is because their motivation involves either seeking to discover a new application for existing or emerging technology, or alternatively, they believe the focus should be about researching a new approach to solving a known problem. As a consequence, they will tend to postpone any consideration of the commercial viability of their idea until progress has been achieved about validating that technology is capable of providing a viable solution. Even at this stage, the entrepreneur will often initiate market entry on the basis of strong self-belief or intuition that an adequate level of customer demand will eventually emerge (Gregoire and Shepherd 2012).

Playbook Guideline 14: Do not expect market research to define a technological opportunity because, often, nobody has any idea that market demand exists

Exploiting Latent Need

Case Aims: To illustrate how a technical solution provided the basis for an entirely new market opportunity

Kozo Ohsone, the head of Sony's tape recorder division, exhibited the classic technological entrepreneurial philosophy of putting development of technical or scientific solutions ahead of market opportunity. His attitude was reflected in the development of a light-weight miniature recorder that permitted the user to listen to music through headphones, but which could not record. Akio Morito, the Sony Chairman, perceived the intrinsic appeal of a portable device offering excellent sound quality, and despite others inside the company concerned about the lack of a recording capability, Morito authorized the creation of a production operation to manufacture what was to become known as the Sony Walkman (Beamish 1999).

Upon market introduction, major Japanese retailers were not enthusiastic, believing that there would be no customer demand for what they perceived was a miniature tape recorder that did not record. Within a few weeks of launch, some very creative marketing activities, aimed primarily at young people, generated a high level of word-of-mouth interest, which soon resulted in massive market demand. The reason for the Walkman's success was the product was personal and portable, untethered from a fixed location, thereby delivering freedom of listening in any situation. As such, it created a new market that would at a later date be exploited by products such as Apple's iPod.

Playbook Guideline 15: Focus on developing a viable technological solution and postpone thinking about market opportunity until later

Creating a Technical Solution

Case Aims: To illustrate how developing a new solution provided the basis for creating a highly successful business.

British entrepreneur James Dyson is motivated to finding new technological solutions to known problems. He identified that the problem with conventional vacuum cleaners is as the bag fills with dust, the suction power declines. Observing in an industrial sawmill a cyclonic separator for removing dust from the air, he believed the same concept could work in a vacuum cleaner. It was this idea that led to the development of his world-beating invention, the Dual Cyclone bagless vacuum cleaner (Anon 2006).

Developing the final product took five years of and involved testing 5,127 prototypes. He showed his final prototype to makers of domestic appliance manufacturers. They were not interested (Schaer 2015). Eventually, he decided to manufacture the product himself. Once in production, Dyson soon discovered the lack of interest among appliance manufacturers was matched by the same level of disinterest among major UK retailers. Hence, he was only able to get distribution in two mail order catalogs and a few small independent retailers. Eventually, the breakthrough finally came in 1995 when Dyson, through a personal contact, was able to achieve distribution in Comet, a large UK retailer.

Playbook Guideline 16: Recognize that persistence is a necessary attribute for technological entrepreneurial success

Foresight

Having established a successful business based on a technological entrepreneurship, the problem is how to avoid being overtaken by changes in technology or by new market entrants. The widely utilized conventional approach to use strategic planning to define future action is of little use when seeking to respond to major changes. This is because the approach is based on extrapolating past events (Farrington, Henson, and Crews 2012).

To avoid being overtaken by technological or scientific advances requires foresight about new technologies, market trends, and the activities of potential competitors. Foresight involves scanning the external environment and provides the basis for identifying new trends, drivers, uncertainties, and other key factors of future influence. This knowledge can guide future entrepreneurial technological developments; thereby avoiding the risks associated with failing to act in time to avoid to losing market leadership (Zahra and Bogner 1999).

Within the German biotechnology industry, Metzner and Reger (2009) identified foresight as being critical in the early identification of emerging trends within the German biotechnology industry. The evolution of the industry has been reliant upon the formation of close collaborative relationships between universities and business. The founders of biotechnology companies are typically academics. Linkages with universities are associated with a firm's innovative outputs. These links are reliant upon formal and informal R&D discussions, attendance at scientific conferences, and analysis of academic publications. Many of the early customers of these firms are scientists or scientific institutions involved in publicly financed research projects. Close existing relationships with such customers provide access to knowledge of leading-edge, new technological or scientific outcomes, permitting the early identification of commercial potential well ahead of competition.

Playbook Guideline 17: Remain in close contact with the individuals who are the leaders in their fields of science or technology

Networks

New knowledge acquisition in entrepreneurial organizations often occurs as a result of informal and formal networking. This can be contrasted with the market-driven organizations where the focus is on the collection and systematic analysis of market data and monitoring competition. Unfortunately, data from market sources tends to emerge at a very late phase in the scientific and technological processes associated with the launch of next generation of products. Hence, reliance upon market sources may severely hamper trend identification, thereby placing the organization in the unenviable situation of launching a "me too" proposition after competition has already established a strong market share for their new product or service (Uotila and Ahlqvist 2008).

In the entrepreneurial organization, individuals, such as lead scientists, acquire information from their participation in formal and informal networks. These information gatekeepers are very active networkers, involved in activities such as being members of relevant national committees, assisting the organization of major academic conferences, and interacting with funding agencies and politicians. However, where foresight activities are the sole preserve of gatekeepers, there is the risk that their control over information access and opportunities may create an excessively powerful influence over trend identification and the selection of R&D programs inside the organization (Hervas-Oliver and Albors-Garrigos 2014).

Playbook Guideline 18: Ensure there is democracy of opinion within the organization to avoid one single individual determining all entrepreneurial development activities

The activities of individual firms may be accompanied by government-sponsored foresight programs. The aim of these projects is to identify opportunities for exploiting science and technology as the basis for enhancing the future prospects for national economic growth. The typical structure of such schemes is to draw upon the expertise among leading academics and industrialists to examine the emerging trends and to recommend which areas of R&D should receive priority in relation to government funding (Calof and Smith 2009). The potential drawback is that, the selected advisors may be influenced by their bias for and against certain areas of science, technology, or sector of industry. It can also be the case that the government may favor "near-to-market" opportunities. This philosophy can be detrimental to adequate funds remaining available for pure science or "blue sky" technology, which has the potential to provide the foundations upon which to build totally new sectors of industry.

Playbook Guideline 19: Be prepared to go you own way when opinions and plans being articulated by others seem incorrect or uninformed

Exploiting Foresight

Case Aims: To illustrate how one high-tech company sustains a leadership position in the face of major shifts in technology

John Chambers, CEO of the American firm Cisco, joined the company at an important moment, namely the startpoint of the Internet revolution. The company as the market leader in switches and connectors was well placed to exploit newly emerging technological entrepreneurial opportunities. Chambers brought with him experience gained while employed at IBM and Wang. These experiences showed Chambers that when large companies have a significant market share, they are often tempted to ignore emerging market disruptions, and instead, focus on using current technology in seeking to continue to grow existing markets (Chambers 2015).

In the case of the Internet, Chambers recognized that firms such as Lucent, Nortel, and Alcatel were continuing to focus on telecoms and the use of fiber optics to transmit data via telephone lines. He understood that the Internet would totally change data interchange technologies and presented new opportunities for Cisco. The company's subsequent development activities have responded to opportunities such as the shift from desktop computers to laptops, smartphones, and tablets, and the move by organizations from owning their own server systems to outsourcing their data storage to the cloud. Cisco's most recent move has been to exploit the emergence of the "Internet of everything" involving fundamental technological shift toward the creation of new online communication channels for numerous, new kinds of devices.

Cisco has created a number of different ways of responding to emerging technological change. One approach is for the firm to engage in R&D to develop new technologies. The second approach involves their "Entrepreneurs in Residence" program. This provides financial support, mentoring, and collaboration opportunities to early-stage entrepreneurs working in areas where Cisco perceives huge future potential. The third pathway is acquisition of a smaller company, which provides access to the knowledge and capability currently not available within Cisco. For example, in 2005, the company Cisco acquired Airespace to accelerate its leadership in the field of Wi-Fi connections. A fourth approach is what Cisco calls a "spin-in." This involves assembling a group of engineers and developers from the existing workforce to work on a specific project and moving them out of the company's mainstream activities in order to create a start-up environment.

Cisco does not always make the right decisions (Mehta, Schlosser, and Hjelt 2001). Sometimes, their foresight approach results in incorrect identification of the potential for exploiting a new technology. In other cases, the company has commenced R&D too early in relation to the emergence of actual market opportunities. For example, the company started work of the "Internet of things" only to discover the market was not yet at the point where there was any significant emerging demand. Their decision, however, was to sustain expenditure until actual market opportunities began to generate revenue.

Chamber's (2015) summarized the company's approach to foresight by saying *"By the time it's obvious you need to change, it's usually too late. Very often you have to be willing to make a big move even before most of your advisers are on board. You have to be bold And you need a culture that lets you figure out how to win even without a blueprint."*

Playbook Guideline 20: Early movers exploit foresight to generate greater wealth than later entrants into the same market

Collaborative Orientation

Conventional marketing management practices usually place strong emphasis activities to combating competitive threats and the protection of market share. This operational philosophy is exemplified by the regular outbreaks of brand wars such as Macdonald's versus Burger King or Pepsi versus Coca-Cola. Such real-world scenarios have resulted in some academic texts continuing to primarily focus on managing the processes associated with attacking and responding to competition (McKelvey 2006).

Evidence of a different managerial philosophy was first identified by the Nordic business schools in the 1970s (Hjorth 2008). In their research on business-to-business (B2B) markets, it was found that in many cases, success was strongly influenced by companies exhibiting a collaborative orientation. Research on the behavior traits of small business owner or managers also revealed a similar orientation (Dubini and Aldrich 1991). This form of collaboration is based on trust, self-interest, and reciprocity.

The existence of strong network relationships is not just important at start-up, but may become even more critical as a new enterprise seeks to achieve business growth (Jarvenpaa and Välikangas 2014).

The complexity of a successful outcome for an entrepreneurial project within high-tech industries is complicated by the reality that, rarely no one single firm has the knowledge and expertise to autonomously resource the total project. As a consequence, collaboration in high-tech sector in recent years has become a critical component in terms of increasing the probability for project success (Chaston 2016).

Playbook Guideline 21: Collaborators are more likely to enjoy sustained success than loners when engaged in technological entrepreneurship

Collaborative Development

Case Aims: To illustrate the important role of entrepreneurial collaboration in the development of new, more technologically advanced next-generation products

The development of new or next-generation products involving complex technologies can rarely occur without a manufacturer working closely with other members of the supply chain. Furthermore, the key objectives within the development process may demand a radical change. The may be due to the emergence of new technology or customer demand shifts, which require development of new technological solutions (De Haan and Mulder 2002).

The success of any new aircraft design is critically dependent on close co-operation between the manufacturers, engine designers, and the availability of materials and subsystems around which the airframe can be constructed (Epstein 2014). By the 1980s, in the face of rising cost of fuel, the airline industry began to face problems sustaining profitability. Furthermore, as the number of aircraft increased in the skies over major metropolitan areas, there were increasing problems over jet noise. Overcoming these two factors demanded further advances in technology to increase operating efficiencies and reduce noise levels.

Initially, the primary focus was on the development of the next generation of more fuel-efficient and quieter jet engines, requiring ongoing co-operation within the aerospace supply chain. The solution was to improve the engine "bypass" ratio, which enhanced fuel efficiency and reduced engine noise (Varga and Allen 2006).

The increasing size of turbofans demanded much stronger wings, which in turn increased aircraft weight and reduced fuel efficiency. This problem necessitated new technological solutions involving the development of lighter materials to replace reliance upon the ongoing use of aluminum (Lind 2006). As with most new technologies, the successful utilization of advanced composites demanded radical innovation in the formulation of these new materials and the development of the manufacturing tools needed to produce such as complete aircraft wings or tail planes. The manufacturers are claiming that their latest generation of aircraft, which incorporate these new materials such as the Boeing 787 Dreamliner, has the weight savings which offers a 20 percent improvement in fuel efficiency.

Entrepreneurial Self-Efficacy

Self-efficacy refers to an individuals' conscious belief in their own ability to successfully undertake a particular task (Bandura 1997). It is an important determinant of human behavior. Individuals tend to avoid tasks about which they have low self-efficacy, while being drawn toward tasks about which they have high self-efficacy. Individuals with a strong sense of self-efficacy in a given domain are likely to approach difficult problems in that domain with persistence and are less likely to be deterred by high levels of complexity.

Chen, Greene, and Crick (1998) developed the construct of entrepreneurial self-efficacy (ESE) to describe the degree to which individuals believe that they are capable of performing the tasks associated with new venture management. Forbes (2005) noted that ESE can influence an individual's willingness to engage in entrepreneurship and the behavior of those who are already entrepreneurs. ESE affects potential entrepreneurs, because individuals' intentions to found new businesses are a function of the extent to which they perceive that it is both feasible and desirable to progress a specific business idea (Krueger and Brazeal 1994). In the case of existing businesses, ESE can influence the willingness to engage in further innovative activities. Additionally, ESE can influence how well entrepreneurs in existing businesses discharge their responsibilities as managers of new projects. In contrast, low levels of self- efficacy are associated with performance-inhibiting behaviors, such as indecision, distraction, and procrastination. Furthermore, individuals with high levels of ESE are better able to recognize new opportunities as these emerge.

Playbook Guideline 22: Strong self-efficacy is a critical attribute for a successful technological entrepreneur

ESE Exemplar

Case Aims: To illustrate how entrepreneurial success breeds even stronger entrepreneurial self-confidence

Involvement in successful ventures such as PayPal permitted Elon Musk to entertain his entrepreneurial dream of becoming involved in space research with his ultimate aim of creating a settlement on the planet Mars (Williamson 2014). Having visited Moscow to determine the cost of purchasing rockets from the Russians, Musk decided he could build more affordable rockets. He estimated that by applying vertical integration and modular approach to software engineering, it would eventually be possible to reduce launch prices by a factor of 10 and still enjoy a 70 percent gross margin in renting out this capacity to others. This resulted in Musk founding his new entrepreneurial venture SpaceX, which has the long-term goal of creating a spacefaring civilization (Kluger 2012).

Musk is the CEO of the Hawthorne, a California-based company. SpaceX develops and manufactures space launch vehicles. Within seven years, SpaceX designed the family of Falcon launch vehicles and the Dragon multipurpose spacecraft. In September 2009, SpaceX's Falcon rocket became the first privately funded liquid-fuelled vehicle to launch a satellite into the earth's orbit (Knapp 2012). SpaceX was awarded a contract from the National Aeronautics and Space Administration (NASA) in 2006 to develop and test a new launch vehicle for transporting cargo to the International Space Station (ISS). In 2012, the SpaceX Dragon vehicle berthed with the International Space Station, making history as the first commercial company to launch and berth a vehicle on the ISS. SpaceX is the largest private producer of rocket motors in the world and holder of the record for highest thrust-to-weight ratio for any known rocket motor.

Musk's other passion is to develop solutions to the growing problem of global warming, and in 2004, became a major investor in the Tesla company (Stringham, Miller, and Clark 2015). Initially intending to avoid involvement in day-to-day operations, his perception of the technological and managerial weaknesses within the company's senior management team caused Musk to assumed leadership of the company as the new CEO. Tesla's first product was the electric sports car, the Tesla Roadster. Subsequently, the company developed and launched their four-door Model S sedan. In addition to focusing on expanding the company product range, Tesla also sells electric powertrain systems to companies such as Daimler, Mercedes, and Toyota.

CHAPTER 3

Leaders and Structure

Management Style

The success of organizations is critically dependent on the presence of an effective leader. Significant research effort has been expended on seeking to identify the behavioral traits that can distinguish between effective and ineffective leaders. Unfortunately, the outcome of this type of research is that, although important leadership traits have been identified, it has not proved possible to specify a universal model upon which to determine the overall effectiveness. This is because individuals have been found to exhibit different traits, but remain effective (Gehring 2007).

One solution to this dilemma has been to focus on the more generic issues of attitudes and behaviors as the basis for identifying different leadership styles and how these influence the organization. One major difference is that, which exists between transactional and transformational leaders (Sashkin and Rosenbach 1998). Transactional leadership focuses on behaviors related to basic administrative and management tasks required for groups to function well in stable environments. In contrast, transformational leadership is based on the ability to recognize followers' needs, demands, and motivation plus how to satisfy the followers' higher-level needs in a way that utilizes the full potential of these individuals. As a consequence, transformational leaders are more effective at creating and supporting a change, which is the reason why many technological entrepreneurial leaders exhibit a transformational style.

Sashkin and Rosenbach posited the critical characteristics of transformational leadership are self-confidence and being a visionary. In terms of fulfilling the latter role, it requires an ability to develop intuitive insights about the future based on limited or even no information.

The behavioral traits of transformational leaders include being creative and credible. These latter traits involve focusing on trust-building, caring, empowerment, and creating opportunities for all employees to maximize their contribution to the organization. Visionary leaders appreciate that their vision must align with the organization's entrepreneurial capabilities in order that the organization is able to fulfill the key attributes of being proactive, innovative, and risk-taking (Ilies, Judge, and Wagner 2006).

The characteristics of a transactional leadership style are that authority and accountability reside within the leader who exhibits a controlling, top-down approach. Most entrepreneurship studies conclude that this is an inappropriate style for educating, inspiring, and energizing the workforce. Furthermore, it may create an environment where employees fear speaking out and are unwilling to be involved in decision making or becoming self-responsible.

Playbook Guideline 23: Senior successful technological entrepreneurs are likely to exhibit a transformational leadership style

Technological Visionaries

Case Aims: To illustrate how individuals who exhibit an entrepreneurial leadership style that results in the creation of new global businesses

United States' move to become the world's wealthiest nation in the late 19th century was assisted by being the home of a number of technological entrepreneurs. Included in the list of individuals with the technological foresight whose endeavors led to the creation of new global industries are Thomas Edison, Henry Ford, and Tom Watson Jr.

Edison was an amazingly prolific identifier of new technologies. His initial focus was on improving telegraph technology. From there, he moved onto to creating the phonograph and the carbon microphone. The technology that spawned most of his patents was in the field of electricity. A key reason for Edison's success was that he established the world's first industrial research laboratory in Menlo Park, New Jersey. He created this new institution with the specific purpose of achieving technological innovation. Like other entrepreneurial technologists, he relied heavily upon intuition to guide his decisions on which problems should be researched. In most cases, the research focused on opportunities for which initially there was little or no evidence of market demand (Vandervert 2011).

Henry Ford's first attempt at creating a manufacturing business was the Detroit Automobile Company. However, the cars produced were of a lower quality and a higher price than Ford wanted. Backed by a new group of investors, he went onto establish the Ford Motor Company, and in 1908, launched the world's first mass production car, the Model T. To achieve the aim of manufacturing the affordable motor car, Ford and his team of engineers created the first car plant that utilized mass production manufacturing techniques (Link 2014).

Tom Watson Jr. became the CEO of IBM company shortly before his father's death in 1956. Until that time, IBM was dedicated to manufacturing electromechanical punchcard systems for managing data. Tom Watson Sr. had repeatedly rejected electronic computers as overpriced and unreliable. As the new CEO, Jr. hired a large number of electrical engineers and assigned them the task of designing mainframe computers at a time when most existing employees did not think computer products were a commercially viable proposition (Watson and Petre 1990).

The first development IBM 7030 Stretch was a not a commercial success, but the knowledge gained provided the basis to the next generation of products. Then, in 1964, IBM introduced the revolutionary System/360, the first of a large family of computers to use interchangeable software and peripheral equipment. Within two years, the System/360 became the dominant mainframe computer in the marketplace, so dominant, in fact, that its architecture became the industry standard.

Playbook Guideline 24: Successful technological entrepreneurs are likely to perceive that scientific or technological problems can be eventually solved

Role Fulfillment

Gupta, MacMillan, and Surie (2004) perceived entrepreneurial leadership role as engaging in "scenario enactment" and "cast enactment." These researchers presented scenario enactment as envisaging possible opportunities that can be exploited through new, unconventional solutions. Cast enactment involves assembling resources, including committed employees to deliver the identified scenario. A risk entrepreneurial leader scan run is that of pushing their team beyond the limits of their capabilities. Hence, the entrepreneurial leader will be forced to balance their desire for aggressive improvement with a pragmatic understanding of the capabilities of their team. This requires combining highly ambitious goals with insightful understanding of the limits of what can be accomplished (Chen 2007).

Playbook Guideline 25: Successful technological entrepreneurs require the ability to understand and inspire others

Entrepreneurial leaders must be able to anticipate and overcome potential resistance to their ideas. This will involve sustaining support from key stakeholders, both inside and outside the firm. A necessary skill is to inspire and mould a team that is highly committed to accomplishing the leader's aims. Goldsmith (2010) posited that, to be successful, entrepreneurial leaders must avoid (i) the urge to win all battles, (ii) excessive stubbornness, (iii) punishing the messenger, and (iv) exhibiting goal obsession.

Playbook Guideline 26: Successful technological entrepreneurs must be able to carry their team with them, especially in the face of adversity

Swiercz and Lydon (2002) proposed two phases of entrepreneurial leadership: the formative growth phase and the institutional growth phase. They concluded that the transition between these two phases can be difficult because the entrepreneurial CEO has to learn to depend upon others, which involves developing a new set of leadership competences. The researchers classified these required competences into "self-competences" and "functional competences." Self-competences include intellectual integrity, promoting the company rather than self, utilizing external advisors, and creating a sustainable organization. Functional competences are essential for successfully performing the challenging tasks and roles of

Table 3.1 Role change*

Start-up leadership tasks	Organizational leadership tasks
Idea seeker	Leveraging resources to support existing ideas and identifying a new idea
Leveraging resources to support existing ideas and identifying a new idea	Leveraging resources to support existing ideas and identifying a new idea
Creating a viable new business	Building a more complex organizational structure while sustaining entrepreneurial capabilities
Leading and inspiring a small team	Developing structures that ensure others take leadership role within individual teams
Fostering limited resources	Ensuring resources remain appropriately allocated to ensure ongoing entrepreneurial activities

* Modified from Swiercz and Lydon 2002.

leading an entrepreneurial venture. The differences between the two roles are summarized in Table 3.1.

Playbook Guideline 27: To sustain their leadership role, technological entrepreneurs must revise their leadership role as their organization grows, by relying upon delegation and increased team member autonomy

Communication

Once an organization has progressed beyond the start-up stage, the entrepreneurial leader needs to develop the skills of listening, communicating, building trust, and exhibiting respect for the dignity and the creative potential of each person within the organization. The outcome is an organization in which change, value enhancement, and entrepreneurial orientation are the norms (Darling and Beebe 2007).

An aspect of successful communication is the effectiveness and appropriateness of the message. The message should be understood as the communicator intended. Message acceptance usually only occurs where the leader is trusted. This will be determined by the degree to which the entrepreneur is predictable, their opinions are well known and are consistent. Where the freedom of choice is acceptable within an organization, both the entrepreneurial leader and the employees should have the right to choose. Freedom of choice will enhance the degree of respect that employees hold about the leadership. Enhancing respect is achieved through the skill of effective listening.

Playbook Guideline 28: Technological entrepreneurs must have the ability to be effective, persuasive communicators and just as importantly, being competent listeners

The Dark Side

Entrepreneurs tend to be achievement-oriented, like to take responsibility for decisions, stay in control, and tend to avoid routine work. Such individuals can usually inject their highly contagious enthusiasm into an organization, conveying a sense of purpose convincing others of the appeal of working alongside them. Kets de Vries (1985) noted, however, that entrepreneurs may have personality faults that make them hard people to work with. Their bias toward action can result in outcomes that can have adverse organizational consequences. Furthermore, their sense of certainty can result in them rejecting other people's suggestions or expressions of concern about what should be perceived as a high-risk activity. Accompanying this self-certainty, these individuals may actually distrust others, questioning their motivation in suggesting an alternative idea. Conger (1999) concluded that an entrepreneur's excessively strong belief in their own ideas can result in a vision that is possibly not the most appropriate at a specific point in time.

The Risk of Technological Fixation

Case Aims: To illustrate how a leader's incorrect convictions can adversely impact an organization

Edwin Land's invention of the Polaroid camera permitted instant photography to exist and also led to the creation of an alternative business model. This was that of the real profit not being from sales of the camera, but from huge profit margin generated from the sale of film. The model was subsequently described as "a razor-blade strategy" where the profit is not in the razor, but from the sale of razor blades (Hintz 2016).

Polaroid was admired for sustaining a high level of ongoing R&D expenditure. Unfortunately, Land was a dominant figure in the organization, determining what he perceived were areas of future opportunity and in defining the company's research focus. One such example of his influence was on the firm's Polavision product, which the company eventually had to write off $89 million and led to Land's resignation as chairman in 1981. The most dangerous aspect of Land's influence, which was eventually to lead to the closure of the company, was an inadequate understanding of the eventual impact of the newly emerging field of digital photography. Land was firmly convinced that the future for Polaroid Corporation would always be through new developments in chemistry, especially in the area photographic chemistry. Hence, despite the company engaging in research in digital photography, Land's influence did mean the company culture was biased against electronics (Ozanian 1995). Another of Land's convictions was his belief that customers would always want a hardcopy print. This perspective was reflected by the establishment of a research team to develop a "printer in the field," an instant camera that would produce a film-based print from a digital image. The error of this perspective eventually became apparent as people began to store digital images on their camera or download the image to a computer for later viewing.

Playbook Guideline 29: No technology can be expected to go on forever

Working Alongside Entrepreneurs Can Be Uncomfortable

Case Aims: To illustrate that working for visionary entrepreneurs may not always be pleasant experience

Jeff Bezos, the founder of Amazon, is an entrepreneur who excels at having visionary ideas. Having disrupted the concept of retailing by creating his online book-selling operation, he has continued to seek new innovative opportunities for his business operations. Although Bezos is clearly the leader and source of the overall corporate vision, he understands the benefits of granting teams the right to be independent thinkers. He calls this philosophy "distributed innovation." It is an important aspect of the organization's flexible mindset that allows Amazon to identify and exploit new opportunities (Lashinsky, Burke, and Mangalindan 2012).

Although Bezos can be charming and supportive, the alternative aspect of his personality is he can be very unforgiving of anyone who is ill-prepared or he believes is making a mistake (Anon 2013). He has a reputation for sending out "Bezos question mark e-mails" to employees over any issue that concerns him. Entire teams are expected to drop everything and to rapidly respond to a question mark communication. Senior managers have learned to carefully review their answers before they respond to the original e-mail. Such activities are a reflection of the fact that Amazon's culture is accepting of individuals being confrontational. This culture originates with Bezos who believes that, in many cases, the only way to discover the truth is through confrontation.

Playbook Guideline 30: Technological entrepreneurs may be difficult to work with, so a "thick skin" is an important attribute for those working alongside them

Appropriate Structure

Entrepreneurial success is fuelled by creativity, imagination, visionary zeal, and a willingness to move into uncharted waters. However, as organizations grow in size, the tendency among senior managers is to seek order, control, and access to detailed information. The conventional solution is to create a hierarchical structure based on layers of management, with specialist managerial tasks assigned to specific departments such as marketing or manufacturing. However, as the world has become a more volatile place with new technologies challenging conventions, these management systems can become a barrier to sustaining a competitive advantage (Ghoshal and Barlett 1995).

Within hierarchical structures, information and decision requests flow upward to the top of the organization; thereby enabling corporate executives to make decisions, assign resources, determine levels of responsibility, and retain control. In these vertically driven, financially oriented organizations, authority-based processes may dominate, thereby acting as a block on horizontal communication processes across departmental boundaries. The most deleterious effect of the growth of bureaucratic structures within corporations is the erosion of entrepreneurship with employees no longer exhibiting externally oriented, opportunity-seeking attitudes. Employee-led initiatives rarely survive because top managers believe they are the best visionaries and should remain responsible for leading their companies in new directions. Employees' ideas are likely to be crushed in the documentation, review, and approval processes that senior managers demand prior to approving the commencement of any new projects (David 1995).

The Benefits of Rule Breaking

Case Aims: To illustrate the steps needed to accelerate innovation in a hierarchical organization

Tom Watson Jr., as well as spearheading the development of the mainframe computer that made IBM so successful, was also the architect of the firm's highly structured hierarchical organizational system. The drawback to this approach in the face of technological change was demonstrated by the company's failure to recognize the growing importance of minicomputers. To avoid the same outcome with the advent of the PC, the company's highly unusual solution was to give approval to Bill Lowe, the Boca Raton Florida laboratory director, the freedom to act autonomously to work on developing a new PC. (IBM archives, accessed 2015).

Lowe claimed his group could develop a small, new computer within a year. He appointed a small team to develop a specification covering hardware, software, manufacturing, and marketing. It was decided that to meet deadlines, the group had to stick to the plan of using tested vendor technology, a standardized, one-model product, open architecture and use outside sales channels for quick consumer market penetration. These decisions meant the team would be breaking the company's product development rules and procedures. To create the operating system and software, the team linked up with Bill Gates of Microsoft. They agreed with his idea that instead of selling IBM his operating system, Microsoft would license the system to the company. To create a sufficiently powerful data-processing capability, it was decided to break with current procurement rules and to adopt an Intel 8088 microprocessor. By breaking all of the company product development rules, the team created the IBM PC within 12 months. At that time, this was the fastest "idea to market launch" project in the company's history.

Playbook Guideline 31: Sometimes, the only solution is to ignore or break existing organizational rules

Organic Structures

Recognition of the problems created by hierarchical organizations has led to the emergence of the alternative perspective that to sustain an entrepreneurial orientation requires the adoption of an organic structure (Miller 1983). This involves creating much flatter structures by removing layers of management, delegating decisions downward to frontline employees, and promoting high levels of horizontal and vertical information flows. Authority is vested with those who have the appropriate expertise. The work process is typically based around small teams who have the expertise to identify problems and develop solutions.

Keeping an organic organization on track is no simple process. It is critical, therefore, that there is an organizational culture that is orientated toward co-operation, collaboration, and a commitment to solving whatever problems emerge (Covin and Slevin 1990). A recognized benefit of start-ups is their small size permits a rapid and flexible response. To replicate these benefits within large organizations usually requires the utilization of an organic structure constituted of small autonomous teams. A key aim of senior management is to ensure there is an effective flow of knowledge both vertically and horizontally within the organization.

Playbook Guideline 32: Organic structures are more likely to lead to entrepreneurial success

Exploiting Autonomy

Case Aims: To illustrate how a belief in empowerment and autonomy can sustain entrepreneurial success

A classic example of a large entrepreneurial firm that is committed to the concept of autonomous entities is 3M, a manufacturer of abrasives and adhesives. At 3M, respect for the individual as an unquestioned article of faith was first articulated by William L. McKnight, the company's leader from 1929 to 1966. Another of McKnight's belief was the company is best served when management trusts those with direct knowledge of the market, internal operations, or the technology, which can lead to innovation. This view, accompanied by a belief in people and recognition that mistakes should be both expected and accepted, has rewarded 3M with thousands of breakthrough entrepreneurial initiatives (Coyne 2001).

Another important aspect of the company philosophy is the expectation that change will continually occur, accurately predicting future markets is rarely possible, and hence, there is a need for ongoing adaptation. This perspective requires the company to continually be undergoing change and a perspective that the majority of sales will come from products that have only been developed in the last few years. To achieve this goal, 3M empowers employees and an understanding that leaders who seek excessive control over an innovation projects will fail.

Recognition of the importance of exploiting new knowledge means there is strong emphasis on communication and knowledge sharing in order that new discoveries can to be fully exploited. To maximize entrepreneurial thinking, employees have the option of engaging in self-directed activities for 15 percent of their time. They can work on projects of their own choosing, their own design, and without management approval. Senior management at 3M views their organization as growing from the bottom-upward through the utilization of small project teams (Ghoshal and Barlett 1995).

Senior management has created mutual dependence and reciprocity within the organizational environments. At 3M, technologists in more than 100 laboratories around the world work openly with one another without secrecy, protectiveness, or the "not-invented-here" syndrome, which often inhibits free exchange of ideas in other companies. As a result of the many knowledge-exchange channels that 3M has created, the company has grown from its base of expertise in abrasives and adhesives to develop a portfolio of more than 100 different technologies. It is the company's well-oiled technological entrepreneurial competence-building process that has become a hallmark of 3M's ongoing success.

Playbook Guideline 33: Technological entrepreneurs perform better when granted the freedom to make their own decisions

Ambidextrous Organizations

Innovation can be exploitative or explorative. The former is incremental in nature, undertaken with the purpose of meeting the needs of existing customers or markets (Benner and Tushman 2003). Explorative innovations are radical and designed to meet the needs of emerging customers or new markets. March (1991) opined that exploitation is about efficiency, control, certainty, and variance reduction, whereas exploration is about search, discovery, autonomy, and innovation. He expressed the opinion that the basic problem confronting an organization is to engage in sufficient exploitation to ensure its current viability, and at the same time, devote enough energy to exploration to ensure its future long-term viability.

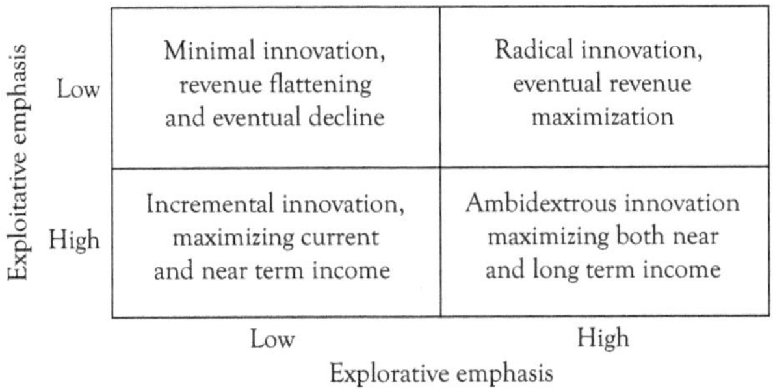

		Low	High
Exploitative emphasis	Low	Minimal innovation, revenue flattening and eventual decline	Radical innovation, eventual revenue maximization
	High	Incremental innovation, maximizing current and near term income	Ambidextrous innovation maximizing both near and long term income

Low   High
Explorative emphasis

Figure 3.1 Alternative innovation philosophies

When exploration is a priority, Christensen and Overdorf (2000) proposed the approach of complementing traditional organizational practices with the creation of new organizational structures, such as spin-outs and acquisitions, to sustain the exploration-oriented objectives of an innovation strategy. This perspective has led to the view that what is required is an "ambidextrous organization" within which both types of innovation are being exploited (O'Reilly and Tushman 2004). This perspective is reflected in Figure 3.1, which suggests four alternative options and revenue outcomes.

Firms with greater technological capabilities tend to have benefitted from ambidexterity. O'Reilly and Tushman found that, within many ambidextrous organizations engaged in both exploratory and exploitative innovation, these activities usually occur in structurally independent organizational units, but which remain strategically integrated within the senior management hierarchy. The different nature of the two types of innovation does mean that conflicts may arise. The likelihood of conflict is further exacerbated by the fact that different senior managers' teams are responsible for exploratory or exploitative organizational units. This can lead to self-interested behavior in which senior managers perceive direct competition with their senior colleagues when it comes to decisions over the allocation of scarce resources. Clearly, such tensions must be avoided, while concurrently, there is emphasis on achieving cross-fertilization and synergies between the various business units. For this to occur requires a need of common vision, with everybody understanding the critical need for both types of innovation, a culture based on collaboration and an accepted managerial trait of seeking to avoid conflict between different units within the organization.

Playbook Guideline 34: Ambidextrous organizations are difficult to create and operate, but are critical for ensuring long-term success

Ambidextrous Exemplar

Case Aims: To illustrate the operation of an extremely successful ambidextrous organization

Google was founded by Larry Page and Sergei Brin, who met in 1995 while they were PhD students at Stanford University. Their joint interest was in organizing the world's information in a way that could make it universally accessible. The search engine they developed provided the basis for a business idea. In itself, however, the search engine did not generate revenue. This only occurred when they linked their search system to selling online advertising. Even today, this business model remains the core of the company's operations, generating a major proportion of the total revenue (Gertner 2014).

Google's mission is not based on money alone, rather it is also to improve the world. The heart and soul of Google is based on entrepreneurship and innovation. The company has a flat, open organizational structure that supports a highly democratic culture in which employees are encouraged to question things. Strategy tends to come from bottom-up. The founders' commitment to innovation has resulted in the emergence of an effective ambidextrous operation. While incremental innovation continues to be utilized to further enhance their Ad Works operation, the company uses generated revenue to support radical innovation and knowledge expansion through acquisition. An example of this latter approach is Android, which went on to become the Android operating system for Google's smartphone operating system launched in 2008.

The company has a long-term orientation toward the development and launch of new radical innovations. This attitude is reflected in Google's driverless car concept. This project started some years ago, long before the car industry perceived the potential benefits of the technology, and it is only now that the point has been reached where a viable commercially feasible product proposition is beginning to emerge.

A core constituent of the company's radical innovation projects is Google X, which is tasked with making actual objects that interact with the physical world. In addition to being responsible for the driverless car operation, three other important projects are Google Glass, high-altitude Wi-Fi balloons, and glucose-monitoring contact lenses. Usually, there is a preference for the criteria that X projects should exhibit. These are to (i) address a problem that affects millions of people, (ii) utilize a radical solution that has at least a component that resembles science fiction, and (iii) must tap into technologies that are now or very soon will become available.

CHAPTER 4

Opportunity Emergence and Evolution

Discovery

Kirzner (1997) considered an entrepreneur is an individual "alert" to opportunities. He posited that alertness is a key difference between entrepreneurs and nonentrepreneurs. Theories of entrepreneurial opportunity reflect an assumption that entrepreneurs either search to discover opportunities or create opportunities without searching. Alvarez and Barney (2007) opined that discovery and creation should be viewed as two conflicting theories of entrepreneurship.

Discovery is about searching the environment for competitive imperfections brought about by external changes. Creation assumes that opportunities do not necessarily evolve out of preexisting industries or markets. Discovery research emphasizes deliberate search as the primary mode of entrepreneurial discovery. The approach assumes the deliberations of the entrepreneurs are critically important in opportunity identification.

Creation involves actions by the entrepreneur's, which result in opportunity recognition that cannot be known prior to undertaking the activity. Hence, entrepreneurs cannot anticipate the possible outcomes of their actions because the information required has not yet been created. The entrepreneur does not search to find opportunities; they develop their new proposition and observe how customers and markets respond to their ideas. In contrast, discovery assumes competitive imperfections result in exogenous opportunities arising from changes in technology, society, regulatory, or the political environment. These opportunities are objective and observable. Should everybody associated with a particular industry or market know about the opportunities, then they could all become involved in exploiting them. This does not occur because it is only entrepreneurs who differ from the majority through their ability to identify or exploit these opportunities (Edelman and Yli-Renko 2010).

Playbook Guideline 35: Technological entrepreneurs can be expected to emphasize creation over discovery when seeking new opportunities

Support for the perspective that the creative entrepreneurial decision-making process differs from the logical structured planning approach utilized by conventional managers was generated by Sarasvathy's (2001) study of 27 of the United States' most successful entrepreneurs. She termed the conventional approach to decision making as being "causal," being based upon a deductive reasoning in the acquisition and analysis of information. In contrast, entrepreneurs exhibited an intuitive approach she labeled "effectuation."

Sarasvathy posited that effectual logic occurs in the earlier stages of venture creation with a transition to more causal strategies as the new firm moves from uncertainty into a more predictable environment. She noted effectual logic is likely to be most effective in settings characterized by high levels of uncertainty. Effectuation dictates that, in highly uncertain and dynamic environments, target customers can only be defined ex-post as being whoever buys a product or service. Instead of focusing on goals, entrepreneurs are more concerned about those things over which they have control. At the individual level, this includes personal knowledge, skills, and social networks.

Playbook Guideline 36: Successful technological entrepreneurs can be expected to exhibit a high level of self-effectuation

Knowledge

Discovery entrepreneurs often have specific knowledge about exploiting an opportunity they have discovered. One reason is they have acquired specialized knowledge and information. In some industries, this specialized knowledge may be embodied more in human capital than in physical capital. Entrepreneurs in these industries can sometimes take advantage of specialized knowledge acquired from their employers and leave to start their start their own businesses (Chaston 2004).

In addition to knowledge gained from their own experience, individuals looking to exploit discovery opportunities may be able to access additional information. The impact of available information may alert innovators to potential new discovery opportunities. Many of those engaging in discovery will have a clear idea of the potential outcomes associated with exploiting an opportunity. In contrast, entrepreneurs often do not know with any certainty the potential scale of opportunity resulting from their discovery. The range of possible outcomes associated with exploiting a discovered opportunity may suggest a high level of risk. However, by using past industry or market experience, industry-specific technical or market-related knowledge and past experience, innovators can often gauge the riskiness associated with opportunity exploitation (Withers, Drnevich and Marino 2011).

Schumpeter (1954) opined that the possession of idiosyncratic information allows people to see particular opportunities that are not obvious to others. This is because variations in information and knowledge influence individuals to identify different values in a commercial proposition. The question arises why do some individuals discover entrepreneurial opportunities and not others? One answer is people recognize those opportunities related to information and knowledge that they already possess. Each individual's prior knowledge creates a knowledge corridor that results in the recognition of certain opportunities. This occurs because prior knowledge influences the ability to comprehend, extrapolate, interpret, and apply new information in a way that was lacking in information available to others (Von Hippel 1994).

Playbook Guideline 37: Technological entrepreneurs often rely upon new knowledge in the development of their ideas and viable solutions

Shane (2000) posited that prior knowledge moderates the relationship between the attributes of a technology and the recognition of entrepreneurial opportunity. He theorized that (i) any given technological change will generate a range of entrepreneurial opportunities that are not obvious to all potential entrepreneurs, (ii) entrepreneurs may discover these opportunities without searching for them, and (iii) any given entrepreneur will discover only those opportunities related to his or her prior knowledge.

At the heart of new product development is the emergence of something new or novel. Identification of novel information and knowledge is a key input to new product development. Hence, the search that directs attention toward new information and knowledge leads the searcher to develop new behaviors, interactions, strategies, and processes that are useful in new product development. Li et al. (2013) posited that the search process involves two components, namely "search selection," which focuses on the locations that managers select to direct their attention to during search, and "search intensity," which describes the cognitive effort and persistence that managers use when searching. These two dimensions are relevant because attention can be wasted when encountered information search is irrelevant, or alternatively, relevant knowledge is not recognized or examined in detail.

Li et al. employed the notion of "terrain unfamiliarity," "terrain distance," and "terrain source diversity" as key dimensions within search selection. Unfamiliar, distant, and diverse terrains are more likely to contain novel, salient, and vivid information that is more likely to capture searchers' attention. Consequently, such new knowledge is more likely to enable searchers to detect insights and breakthroughs related to radical product innovation. In addition to capturing the searchers' attention better, unfamiliar, distant, and diverse terrains are also more likely to yield new information, which helps searchers update their knowledge base and gain insights into the detection, development, and deployment of new products.

Playbook Guideline 38: New knowledge provides technological entrepreneurs with insight and breakthroughs that provide the basis for radical innovation

Smith et al. (2005) found the rate of new product introduction to be a function of knowledge workers' ability to combine and exchange information. They determined that novel information enables firms to develop new ideas about how to allocate resources better and how to co-ordinate innovation efforts. Furthermore, novel information allows firms to discard obsolete knowledge. This is critical because replacing obsolete knowledge can help reduce the possibility of firms becoming trapped in behavior based on competences developed and used in the past.

Search intensity has an important influence on the success of innovation outcomes. Gregoire and Shepherd (2012) suggested that where managers stop gathering information after finding a satisfactory alternative, they may remain ignorant of better alternatives. In the context of developing new products, increased search effort and persistence provide searchers with enhanced capacity to notice, interpret, and make sense of information and knowledge in ways that foster the detection, development, and deployment of new products.

Prior Knowledge Diversity

Case Aims: To illustrate how diversity in prior experience will determine the nature of the opportunities identified for a new technology

Three-dimensional printing (3DP™) was developed and patented by MIT in the United States. The process provided the basis for creating a whole new approach to manufacturing technology. Shane (2000) used licenses granted by MIT for this technological breakthrough innovation to examine how different entrepreneurs identified new opportunities for exploiting technology.

All of the entrepreneurs described a discovery process that involved recognition of an opportunity, rather than engage in a search for information upon which to base their new products. Each had heard about the technology from someone directly involved in development work at MIT and immediately recognized a potential opportunity. When the various commercial outcomes were reviewed with the entrepreneurs, all of them confirmed that they would not have identified the opportunities that the other firms in the sample were pursuing. This was because, in terms of opportunity recognition, all of them drew upon their prior experiences and knowledge of a specific industry or market sector.

Discontinuity

In many industries, there are long periods where there is little change other than incremental technical improvement. However, there can be periods when discontinuities emerge, which are fundamentally different and reflected in order-of-magnitude improvements in the cost or quality of the product (Anderson and Tushman 1990). These product discontinuities are fundamentally different product forms that provide the basis for entrepreneurial technological change. Examples include the jet versus piston engines, diesel versus steam locomotives, CT scanners versus x-rays, and integrated circuits versus discrete transistors.

Anderson and Tushman characterized technological discontinuities as competence-enhancing or competence-destroying. The impact of a discontinuity is the greatest when there is a radical advance in technology. In many cases, the early form of radical innovation is crude, but nevertheless will result in technological uncertainty. This period of uncertainty is characterized by two selection processes, namely competition (a) between existing and new technical regimes and (b) within the new technical regimes. This period of substantial uncertainty eventually ends with the emergence of a dominant technology.

Competition between old and new technologies can be fierce. The new technologies may be criticized because they frequently perform poorly or demand new competences that are inconsistent with the existing established technologies. This criticism is often accompanied by an increase in the level of innovativeness among firms committed to an existing technology. Concurrent with competition between old and new technologies is competition between the supporters of the new technology. This is reflected in the emergence of several entrepreneurial versions of the new technology that appear. This occurs because the technology is not well understood, and each pioneering firm has an incentive to differentiate their variant from their rivals. This latter type of competition often results in initial designs rapidly improving as the innovators gain understanding of the new technology and the nature of market demand.

Anderson and Tushman concluded the length of the era of competition is contingent on the nature of the technological discontinuity. When a technology generates a completely new knowledge base and many rival designs appear, it will take longer for the market to choose the winner. Furthermore, firms confronted with the choice of abandoning existing know-how in the face of competence destroying technical change will defend older technology more stubbornly, prolonging uncertainty about whether the new technology will become dominant. The process of converging on adoption of a new industry standard will be hampered by a lack of common understanding among entrepreneurs about the exact nature of the opportunities created by the new technology. However, once a new dominant design emerges, future technological progress will tend to be based on incremental improvements elaborating upon what is now the accepted industry standard. The emergence of a dominant design permitted firms to move toward standardized and interchangeable parts and the optimization of organizational processes to achieve higher volumes and efficiency. From the customer's perspective, dominant designs reduce product-class confusion and usually result in lower product cost.

During the era of rapid technological innovation, potential customers are confronted with several different versions of the new technology. Choosing any variant in the absence of a standard is risky. Hence, the majority of potential adopters will await the emergence of an industry standard before purchasing a radically different new product or new process technology. This scenario led Anderson and Tushman to argue that the emergence of a standard is a prerequisite to mass adoption and volume production of a new generation of technology.

Playbook Guideline 39: The aim of the technological entrepreneurs is to ensure their radical solution becomes adopted as the new standard within specific industrial sectors or markets

An Industrial Discontinuity

Case Aims: To illustrate how technological discontinuities can impact the performance of organizations

Following the invention of the telephone in the 1870s by Alexander Graham Bell, the core technology, accompanied by incremental innovation, remained virtually unchanged for over 100 years. The technological discontinuity in the 1980s was the development of the mobile phone. Initially, the product was extremely expensive and mainly mounted in cars. Due to high prices, mobile phones were products that initially only appealed to the business market. Motorola in the United States, Ericsson from Sweden, and Nokia from Finland were the dominant players in this new industry (Giachetti and Marchi 2010).

The key influence on market expansion for the mobile phone was the agreement of a standardized system for signal generation in Europe known as the Global System for Mobile Communication (or GSM). This standard created a common bandwidth that would facilitate pan-European roaming, established mass market opportunities, and reduced call costs. GSM became known as second-generation mobile phones (or 2G), and unlike early systems, used digital signal technology. This enabled the development of services, encryption of voice and data, additional capacity, reduction of the size of base stations, and lower prices.

The launch of the digital technology marked two distinct technological discontinuities, namely the sudden redundancy of the first-generation analog devices and the rise of second-generation services and equipment. Nokia committed earlier than competition to the emerging pan-European digital GSM mobile communication standard and started to building relationships with new independent mobile network operators. Size and weight of mobile phones shrank rapidly, which along with commercialization of handsets to the consumer market accelerated by the increasing number of network operators' involvement in consumer markets. To stimulate market expansion, network operators such as Vodafone began to purchase handsets from Original Equipment Manufacturers (OEMs) and then sold them to consumers through retail outlets (Doz and Kosonen 2008).

In the second half of the 1990s, the size, weight, and price of handsets continued to be reduced. During this period, 1990s, Motorola began losing market share mainly, because, despite the growing interest in digital technologies, the company possibly focused on the production and development of analog devices for far too long. As competition intensified, most companies adopted a strategy based on low price (Shi, Chiang, and Rhee 2006). Meanwhile, Nokia, the market leader, maintained a strategy based on exploiting customer replacement demand. Three product technologies drove the replacement cycle, namely multimedia messaging service (MMS), color displays, and camera phones. Japan became the innovation center where top OEMs first tested new technological features. However, weak brand recognition outside their home market resulted in Japanese OEMs unable to gain a first-mover advantage over foreign competitors in overseas markets. Their product innovations became copied and used as a source of product differentiation by the bigger international rivals. At this stage, in order to stimulate the demand for replacement purchases, OEMs added to both low- and high-end handsets and offered new functionalities such as a digital camera, MP3 player, Internet connection, radio, and a voice recorder. By the mid-2000s, these multitasking products had become the new dominant design.

By offering functionalities that are not related to basic voice communication capabilities, these OEMs were entering markets already populated by firms within the computer industry. Hence, some personal computer (PC) makers were prompted to enter the mobile phone market. The most successful was Apple, which launched the iPhone, a device combining voice, MP3 player, and personal digital assistant (PDA) applications to create the smartphone. These are electronic handheld devices that integrate the functionality of a mobile phone, PDA, and other information-exploitation appliances. Although more expensive than the basic mobile phone, the diversity of applications and services delivered has resulted in the smartphone permitting computer firms such as Apple to enjoy huge profits while OEMs such as Nokia faced severe financial difficulties.

Bold Innovation

Once entrepreneurial products enter the market maturity phase, there is a tendency for firms, in the face of increasing competition, to engage in commoditization. Innovation involving line extensions, modifications, and minor performance upgrades become the priority. As a consequence, resources are assigned to new-product development efforts in the wrong areas, namely in flat markets, mature technologies, and tired product categories, which eventually constitute the majority of firm's product portfolio (Chaston 2016).

To avoid this outcome, Cooper (2011) posited that what is required is "bold innovation" involving the firm focusing R&D efforts on the most attractive arenas for future market growth. For this to occur, the firm will need to create a positive climate for entrepreneurial innovation, support radical innovation at every opportunity, and to welcome ideas from all employees. Furthermore, there is the need for having the right senior leadership that can drive and support the innovation effort with words as well as through actions. Unfortunately, many businesses lack the needed climate, culture, and leadership for innovation, and as a consequence, fail to engage in larger scope and more imaginative development projects.

Playbook Guideline 40: Long-term growth demands ongoing commitment to engaging in radical, not incremental, innovation

Cooper noted that generating great ideas is only half the battle. Success also requires that there is an effective rapid idea-to-launch system in place. Additionally, there is the issue that many businesses have lots of good new product ideas, but lack the appetite to invest in larger-scope, more risky projects, despite the fact they promise to be tomorrow's growth engines. Part of the problem can be the lack of a solid business case. This is because big concept projects are innovative and risky. It is difficult to get the accurate data and construct a solid, fact-based business case to convince senior management to make the investment. Senior management should drop their reliance upon financial tools and return-on-investment methods to make their go or no-go decisions. These methods work for smaller, less innovative projects, but may lead to the wrong decisions when it comes to larger-scope, riskier innovation programs. Instead, there is a requirement to assess ideas in relation to fertile strategic arenas identified as likely to offer major new sources of market growth through the development of radically new products or services.

Cooper posited that the potential for success is likely to be much higher when based on a philosophy of attacking from strength. This approach relies upon identifying the firm's unique capabilities that could be leveraged to advantage in other markets, applications, and sectors. He suggested that specification of these strategic areas is fundamental to defining the nature of major new product development efforts. Without this, the search for specific new product ideas or opportunities is likely to remain unfocused, and the portfolio of new product projects can contain a lot of unrelated projects, in many different markets, technologies, or product types.

Playbook Guideline 41: Long-term success often depends on understanding the company's strengths and exploiting these when engaging in radical innovation

Acting Boldly

Case Aims: To illustrate the benefits of recognizing the ongoing validity of returning to an organization's original entrepreneurial competence model

Corning Company began to manufacture glass casings for Thomas Edison's light bulbs in New York in the 19th century. However, it was the entrepreneurial enthusiasm of Eugene Sullivan in the early 20th century that established the vision of the company exploiting an understanding of the chemistry and capabilities of glass to provide the basis for new innovative products. Included in the product line, which subsequently emerged as a result of this vision, were ovenproof ceramics (notably Pyrex and Corning Ware), cathode-ray color TV tubes, and fiber optics for voice and data communication (Kelly 2010).

The huge financial lure of becoming the leading manufacturer of fiber optics for the telecommunications industry caused the company to decide to drop the vision of utilizing research on the chemistry and capabilities of glass to develop new products. The company became deeply involved in production of fiber optics. Initially, this action led to a doubling in annual revenue between 1997 and 2000, caused the company to expand manufacturing capacity, and to fund this strategy, selling off their large medical services business and the Pyrex and Corning Ware operations.

In the early 21st century, changes in the telecommunications industry and the entry of other firms into the fiber optics sector left Corning facing excess manufacturing capacity, declining demand, and an operating loss of $500 million (Mehta 2001). The board persuaded the retired chairman James R. Houghton, the great-great grandson of Coming's founder, to return as the new CEO. He found that the optical fiber group had been receiving the bulk of R&D funds, and other areas of research expertise in the chemistry of glass had been left to wither away. Houghton recognized the need to return to the company's founding competences. He drastically reduced the scale of Corning's fiber optics operations and shut down the firm's new small photonics business. He was also, much to his own personal regret, forced to make thousands of employees redundant.

To rebuild Corning, Houghton chose to return to being a competence-driven, diversified, research-orientated company and to avoid making short-term decisions based purely on financially attraction. Within only a few years, Corning has become a global leader in four market segments, namely display technologies, environmental technologies, telecommunications, and life sciences. The proven importance of R&D is evidenced by the opening, in 2010, of the company's new $300-million research facility at Sullivan Park Research and Development campus in the New York state.

CHAPTER 5

The Macroenvironment

Introduction

The tendency of many individuals and organizations is to focus on factors within their specific core market system perceived as future opportunities or threats. In terms of the influence, these are assumed to come from actions by suppliers, competition, intermediaries, or a shift in the behavior pattern of end users. However, as shown in Figure 5.1, external to the core system are other variables that also represent potential sources of influence on future organizational performance. The key difference between core market and these macroenvironmental factors is the latter are not sector-specific influences. This is because they have a more generic impact, in some cases, influencing the performance of entire economies. The problem is identification and accurately forecasting their impact is more difficult than identifying the potential effect of changes in the core market variables (Liao, Welsch, and Pistrui 2001).

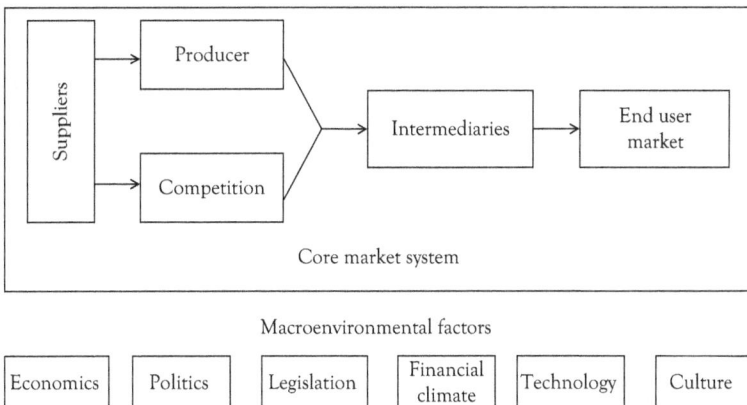

Figure 5.1 A market system model

Economics

A potentially disruptive technological innovation can only succeed when the new proposition generates a profit. In his original formulation of disruptive innovation, Christensen's (1997) perspective was that of market success being achieved by developing a product of service, which although exhibiting a poorer performance than existing established goods, was capable of being offered at a lower price. Although examples such as the minicomputer, the mini-mill, and first-generation PCs provide validation of his theory, the number of successful market entries is somewhat limited. This is because low-end disruption usually does not involve a major investment in new technology, but in most cases, is the outcome of a clever recombination of existing technologies.

Subsequently, it has been accepted that there may also be a potential for disruption by developing a high-end, superior-performance proposition. The reason for high-end market entry is that, developing a new technology is typically a very expensive process. As a consequence, the initial launch will need to be a high-end premium price introduction in order to generate a profit. This situation usually necessitates that prevailing economic conditions permit potential customers to perceive the new proposition is affordable. Even where economic conditions are positive, initially, the new product will tend be perceived a niche product only of interest to a limited number of potential customers.

Although new high-end niche propositions are of minimal concern to companies involved in supplying products or services using existing conventional technology, the potential threat is that should cost reduction through innovation permit a price reduction, then the benefit offered by the new technology will be perceived as affordable by the majority of customers in a market sector. As this juncture, significant market disruption is likely to occur. The outcome for long-established suppliers may be that of declining revenue, which in some cases, may eventually lead to bankruptcy, unless these organizations develop the capability to begin exploiting the new technology.

High-end disruptors' strategy is to produce innovations that are leapfrog in nature, making them difficult to be rapidly imitated. They outperform existing products on one or more critical high appeal benefits at launch, sell for a premium price, and target incumbents' most profitable customers, going after the most discriminating and least price-sensitive buyers before spreading to the mainstream. Examples include Apple's iPod displacing the Sony Walkman, Dyson's bagless vacuum cleaners' impact on the conventional vacuum cleaner manufacturers, and the mobile telephone as these became smaller and cheaper. Existing incumbents did not react fast enough and these high-end disruptors took over their markets (Sandström, Magnusson, and Jörnmark 2009).

High-End Risk

Case Aims: To illustrate the risks associated with investment in high-end technology, which is more expensive than conventional technology

An example of a high-end alternative technology is provided by the development of fracking in the oil and gas industry. This technique was first developed in the late 1940s to stimulate greater output for existing hard-rock wells involving the injection of a pressurized liquid. It was not until the 1980s that producers began experimenting with ways of opening up new wells from oil and gas deposits located in high-permeability rock formations. The new process involves the high-pressure injection of "fracking fluid" constituted of primarily water, sand, or other chemicals to create cracks in deep-rock formations. The entrepreneurial innovation that dramatically expanded access to more difficult deposits was the development of horizontal drilling in place of the more conventional process of vertical drilling.

The drawback with fracking is the breakeven production cost is in the region of $50 a barrel, whereas breakeven for producers in the highly productive Middle East fields is in the region $5 to $10 per barrel. Hence, it was only when oil prices at times significantly exceed $50 per barrel is fracking a commercially viable proposition. Hence, as world prices began to trend upward, there was a major expansion in the use of racking by the oil industry. However, the downturn in the global economy in 2015 caused demand for oil to decline and oil prices fell to below $50 per barrel. Although the price drop affected the total revenue of producers in the Middle East using conventional vertical drilling technology, the impact on the U.S. fracking industry was much more dramatic, with many producers beginning to lose money. This resulted in some wells being shut down and plans for new drilling to be severely curtailed. This situation subsequently proved to be a short-term scenario, and when the OPEC nations decided to curtail the total production, oil prices have begun to rise and the more productive fracking sites are again generating a profit.

Playbook Guideline 42: Opportunities exist for moving from a high-end entrepreneurial niche product to a mass-market positioning when cost reduction or where positive economic conditions permit

Politics

Most Western democracies can be considered as moving through three phases (Bannister and Wilson 2011). During the first phase, which lasted from the mid-1950s until the late 1970s, Western governments engaged in problem solving, market interventionist activities, and the creation of the welfare state. During the 1980s, the "lean state" concept emerged with "big government" going into decline, as politicians sought to reverse many of the changes of the preceding three decades, which had resulted in rapidly rising levels of inflation and public sector labor unrest. The outcome was "new public management" model involving the ideas of privatization, decentralization, hollowing out, managerialism, de-layering, outsourcing, and marketization. More recently, governments have moved into the "activating phase" in which governments have evolved into players in a web of interrelationships between public bodies, state agencies, and organizations.

No matter which phase of process prevails, governments tend to seek to influence economic growth by stimulating innovation in the newer industries, such as biotechnology and computing, using a variety of tools such as grants, soft loans, reduced taxes, and inward investment grants. Although there is variable evidence concerning the impact of such initiatives, the general consensus in the literature is that governments are rarely capable of "picking winners." As a result, successful outcomes have only been achieved in only a minority of cases. Brown and Beynon-Jones (2012) posited a key reason is the susceptibility of government bodies to believe scientific claims by key business stakeholders of a need to react rapidly to often unchallenged claims of the imminent risk of falling behind in global high-tech markets. The researchers believed this behavior trait can be expected to continue to inhibit the opportunity for a government policy to have a major positive impact on leading-edge innovation in their respective countries. In part, this failure can be explained by the relatively short period of time that a politician spends in office, thereby orientated toward projects that appear to offer immediate success before the next electoral cycle.

Based on the research on Japan, Beason and Weinstein (1995) concluded that there is no real economic benefit to be generated by government policy tools aimed at supporting of high-growth industries. In fact, in the case of Japan, it appeared that sectors most favored by government intervention tended to be slow-growth industries. As a consequence, subsidized sectors such as textiles, mining, and steel continued to get bigger. Furthermore, they found the application of industrial sector support tools was highly unsystematic, with some sectors benefiting from one measure and simultaneously suffering from some other contradictory one. The researchers concluded that Japan exhibited traits in relation to supporting innovation very similar to those used by the French and American governments, namely politically driven, favor-based, uniformed, and biased decisions in most cases have been nonhelpful to these nations' respective overall economic performance.

Playbook Guideline 43: Identification and support for specific industries by governments is not very likely to ensure long-term success through engagement in innovation

Legislation

Governmental regulation involves the employment of legal instruments for the implementation of socioeconomic policies. A characteristic of legal instruments is that individuals or organizations can be compelled by government to comply with prescribed behavior under the penalty of sanctions. Corporations can be forced, for example, to observe certain prices, to supply certain goods, to stay out of certain markets, to apply particular techniques in the production process, or to pay the legal minimum wage. Sanctions can include fines, the publicizing of violations, imprisonment, an order to make specific arrangements, an injunction against withholding certain actions, or closing down the business (Van den Bergh 2016).

The "normative theory of regulation" deals with reasons why market failure has necessitated the need for regulations. Failures can range from external effects, natural monopolies, public goods availability, sunk costs, ruinous price war, universal service, interconnection, cross-subsidization, and asymmetrical information in relation to economically important sectors. The regulative instruments for intervening in markets can include barriers to market access and price regulation. Regulation shapes the motivations and abilities, and thus, changes incumbents' behavior. This suggests governmental regulation can be one of the main drivers in some markets because the existence of legislation has the potential to substantially change the motivation and ability of new entrants and incumbents (Christensen, Anthony, and Roth 2004).

Playbook Guideline 44: Technological entrepreneurs need to be aware that government legislation can be a major barrier to achieving commercial success

Government Regulations Impacting Energy

Case Aims: To illustrate how technological innovation can be influenced by governments, instead of a market opportunity

Growing concerns about global warming and the adverse environmental impact of burning pollution-causing fuels, such as coal, have influenced the developed nation governments to focus on the replacement of hydrocarbon energy with renewable resources, such as wind and solar power. Solar firms in some countries are still faced with environmental uncertainty in relation to investing in technological innovation or scaling up their operations. One source of environmental uncertainty arises from firms' inability to predict accurately the future state of governmental policies. The effects include a perceived inability to predict effects of future policy states or the consequences of response to new legislation. Disagreement and uncertainty may also arise from how to implement regulation. For example, in Europe, having announced subsidies for solar energy generation, governments have determined these are too expensive, and subsequently, severely reduced these causing financial problems for both producers and consumers. Another source of uncertainty stems from the relations and interdependence of regulation on solar energy to other energy regulation. (Hoffmann and Busch 2008).

Green (2008) noted that Shell Oil's former President and CEO John Hofmeister, when speaking of the U.S. situation, suggested that America's "energy is politicized." In reality, this statement can be extended to cover most other major nations (e.g., Russia's use of gas pricing to influence the loyalty of East European nations; America's policy only recently revoked of banning oil and gas exports). It is possibly very relevant in the field of renewable energy, as governments have sought to ensure that their domestic firms have obtained a share of this rapidly growing sector within the energy industry. This situation creates a major dilemma for firms committed to a strategy based on the technological entrepreneurship because their success is dependent on responding to government regulations, which may create obstacles in relation to focusing on investing in new technologies capable of achieving long-term market success.

Technology

With an improvement to a well-understood technology or the advent of a totally new technology, firms face the scenario that a technological change can be considered an opportunity or a threat. Hence, tracking a technological change is a critically important. The activity becomes infinitely more difficult in those cases where the new technology originates from outside an industry sector. This is because when a new technology from outside an industry sector incumbent firms often lack the capabilities to exploit this technology (Zahra and George 2002). A classic example of this scenario was the introduction of the microchip in the watch industry severely impacting the majority of existing firms, which continued to use the traditional mechanical clockwork movement in their products.

Incumbents may face the difficult choice about which innovations might sustain performance. When a radical entrepreneurial innovation opportunity arises, the incumbent must weigh the potential benefits of costs and risks versus benefits. A radical innovation may offer the promise of superior performance, but development risks can be high. Hence, commercial returns can be difficult to predict (Chao and Kavadias 2008).

Hill and Rothaermel (2003) opined that, for incumbents, the possibility of new entrepreneurial entry from outside the industry complicates the choice of future innovation pathways. This is because radical innovation may have the potential to supplant, and eventually, overtake existing products. Consequently, this makes radical innovations especially appealing to entrepreneurial entrants as providing a drastic change capable of dislodging existing firms from their dominant industry position.

Available evidence suggests firms to rely on rivals' actions as a source of information about the market potential for radical innovations. Much of the extant literature has examined why incumbents might underinvest or ignore radical innovations. One explanation for such behavior is the lack of incentives to cannibalize revenues from existing products or to replace expensive capita assets associated with exploiting current technology (Chandy and Tellis 1998). Organizational inflexibility and core rigidities of development teams and management have also been identified. There is also the possibility that incumbents have a bias against radical innovation on the basis of inputs from their current customers.

Traditional monitoring processes in nonentrepreneurial companies are largely arbitrary, dependent on what individuals in the company believe. In today's world, such an arbitrary process is insufficient. Hence, to overcome this problem, a number of new techniques, known as technical intelligence (or TI), have been developed (Lichtenthaler 2004). The techniques are based on scanning and monitoring activities linked to a knowledge management system to store, retrieve, and prioritize relevant technological information. For the TI process to be truly effective, there needs to be development of the capability to predict potential technology-based threats and opportunities as well as connecting a company's core competences to relevant technological surroundings.

Playbook Guideline 45: Remaining ahead of competition depends on effective monitoring of technological trends, both inside and outside specific sectors of industry

Meta-Trends

Meta-trends are emerging events or scenarios that will impact entire populations at a national, regional, or global level. The importance of meta-trends is that problems may become apparent, which can only be resolved through entrepreneurial technology. Brown and Flynn (2008) posited that climate change represents, perhaps, the most profound of the many environmental meta-trends expected to impact business in the 21st century. In 2007, the Intergovernmental Panel on Climate Change (IPCC) released the Fourth Assessment Report summarizing a range of impacts and policy recommendations around predicted climate change trends. The report forecasted that climate change will cause more variable weather, heat waves, heavy precipitation events, flooding, droughts, intense storms, and air pollution. Such studies have caused most governments to become concerned about global warming. In turn, this has resulted in grants and subsidies being made available, which has accelerated entrepreneurial activity in areas such as emission reduction in traditional industries and in new renewable energy technologies.

While scientists predict climate change will amplify global stresses over the coming decades, concerns are also rapidly growing about the availability of adequate supplies of freshwater. Currently, agricultural irrigation accounts for 70 percent of global water usage and can represent much as much as 95 percent of the total water use in developing countries. Industry follows next with 22 percent of global water use for energy production, processing, cooling functions, a resource input in many products, and waste disposal. With only 8 percent left for use by the domestic sector, more than one billion people currently have no access to safe drinking water worldwide (United Nations 2003).

The United Nations' prediction is that, by 2025, 1.8 billion people will be living in countries or regions with absolute water scarcity, while two-thirds of the world's population could be living without access to enough clean water to meet their needs. These concerns have resulted in expanded interest in desalination technology, which is an energy-expensive proposition. Hence, research has focused on ways of reducing energy utilization.

The other adverse impact of inadequate water supplies is on agriculture. This has resulted in entrepreneurial activities in two areas. The first has been in the area of improved, more efficient irrigation systems exploiting concepts such as remote location sensors. Accompanying these efforts has been focus on using genetic modification (GM) to develop crops more resistant to limited availability of water (Dascher, Kang, and Hustvedt 2014).

Another meta-trend is that of population ageing that is caused by people living longer and declining birth rates. The outcome is that of people aged 65+ becoming an increasingly dominant component of a nation's population. This has two implications, namely the increase in age-related mental illnesses, such as dementia, and the rising cost of the high labor content process of caring for older people. In relation to mental illness, entrepreneurial opportunities from this meta-event are likely to arise from radically different medical solutions as a consequence of ongoing research into brain mapping and understanding the physiology of nervous system change and deterioration. As far as reducing labor costs, two areas of development are the use of remote sensors to monitor people in their own homes and the introduction of robots to replace the use of human carers (Chaston 2009a).

Playbook Guideline 46: Meta-trends offer excellent opportunities for the identification of problems and the generation of new opportunities for the technological entrepreneur.

CHAPTER 6

Competence

Contrasting Theories

Up until the 1980s, concepts associated with optimizing organizational performance were usually based on the premise that (a) marketing strategy formulation required developing ways of exploiting the opportunities available within the external environment and (b) marketing tactics are determined by the nature and structure of the industry of which the organization is a part. This emphasis on environmental orientation is exemplified by Porter's (1980) "contending forces" model. Critics of environmentalism have expressed concern that excessive emphasis on the external market can be detrimental to organizational performance. This is because reliance on a purely market-orientated strategy without regard to the internal competences necessary to support delivery of products or service performance may lead to an organization being overtaken by competitors who have developed more advanced internal competences, thereby becoming able to offer a superior benefit proposition.

The proposed alternative strategic philosophy that has become known as the "'resource-based view" (RBV) of the firm is based on the idea that, in increasingly competitive markets where all firms understand customer needs, differentiation can only be achieved by organizations focusing on and exploiting some form of superior internal capabilities (or "competences"). The core premise of the RBV theory is achievement of a competitive advantage is reliant upon an organization's ability to organize resources to produce goods and services superior to that of other market participants.

Competence can be considered as an ability to co-ordinate the deployment of available assets to permit an organization to achieve specified strategic goals. Kellermanns et al. (2016) opined that, for any aspect of internal operational activity to be recognized as a competence, it should meet the three conditions of ownership, intention, and goal attainment. Competence building involves any process that leads to changes in existing assets and capabilities or the emergence of new capabilities that support improvement in organizational performance. Ownership of a specific competence does not guarantee attainment of a sustainable competitive advantage. This is because two types of internal resources are necessary to establish a competitive advantage, namely assets and competences. Assets are a firm's accumulated resources such as the existence of certain specialist equipment or manufacturing facilities that are necessary to undertake production processes. In contrast, competences are the accumulated knowledge and skills that enable staff to undertake activities that lead to the most advantageous utilization of the organization's assets.

Hamal and Pralahad (1994) posited that an organization can utilize a core competence to support the development of new and or improved products and/or enter new market sectors (e.g., Apple's move from computing into electronic communication with the iPod, iPhone, and iPad). Alternatively, organizational focus may be directed toward developing superior operational technologies that permit the organization to compete on the basis of superior performance or price (e.g., the U.S. retailer Walmart that exploited superior cost-saving capabilities in the areas of procurement and logistics as the basis for outcompeting other supermarket chains by offering much lower prices to consumers).

Playbook Guideline 47: One source of technological entrepreneurial opportunity is to exploit a superior organizational competence

Coyne, Hall, and Clifford (1997) defined a core competence as "*a combination of complementary skills and knowledge bases embedded in a group or team that results in the ability to execute one or more critical processes to a world-class standard.*" They proposed that competences can be of two types, namely insight/foresight and frontline competences. These authors proposed that frontline competences tend to be more important in service industries where the quality of an end product or service can vary appreciably depending on the activities of frontline personnel. In their view, insight/foresight enables a company to recognize opportunities to develop an entrepreneurial first-mover advantage.

Savory (2006) concluded that the increasing complexity of markets and technology-based organizational processes demand that new or revised competences must deliver "higher-level capabilities." Achievement will involve the organization concurrently analyzing both core competence and market positioning. During implementation of a response, it will frequently be the case that resources will need to be transferred from one area to another within the organization. In relation to matching competences to market circumstances, Kay (2004) proposed there are five major sources of strength available to an organization, namely reputation, innovation competence, internal capabilities, organizational assets, and external relationships. He noted that these strengths will vary from industry to industry and from organization to organization operating in the same industrial sector.

Playbook Guideline 48: Technological entrepreneurial outcomes are enhanced when it is feasible to match market opportunities with an internal core competence

Core Competence Strategy

Case Aims: To illustrate exploitation of competences can support the delivery of the same entrepreneurial marketing strategy over many years

An organization that continues to exploit internal competences to effectively exploit the future is the Japanese corporation Canon. Created 60 years ago, the firm's first core competence was in the area of optics because the firm spent the first 30 years of its life making cameras. In 1962, the decision was made to enter the office equipment market. As Xerox Corporation held patents on photocopying technology and would not grant licenses, Canon drew upon both existing and newly acquired competences to develop new photocopying technology, which did not infringe the Xerox patents. Launched in 1970, their first product the NP-1100 had a number of original features, including the first-ever toner cartridge that vitiated the need for service calls.

Having became the world leader in photocopying machines, the firm then applied existing and newly acquired competences to enter the desktop printer market. Although Hewlett-Packard beat Canon in terms of launching the first low-cost ink-jet printer, Canon has continued to sustain their vision concerning opportunities in electronic printing. One area of focus is in applying ink-jet technology for printing directly onto fabrics. They are now the market leaders in supplying massive printing machines to the clothing and textile industry.

The second, and potentially even larger opportunity, was the creation of a digital camera, which can be linked to a printer without the need for the intervention of a computer. Consequently, consumers can now produce their own photographs without having own a computer or buy film for their camera. This opportunity linked together Canon's competences across the areas of optics, cameras, digital data transmission, and print reproduction, and specialist inks permitted the organization to sustain their strategy of acting entrepreneurially by developing and expanding their extensive line of innovative products.

Watanabe and Ane (2003) concluded that ongoing Canon's success can be attributed to the ongoing utilization of a business strategy based on combining existing and new knowledge to support entrepreneurial diversification. The approach has permitted the development of new functionality by focusing on wide-ranging inter-technology spillovers from indigenous core fundamental technologies and manufacturing processes that have supported broader involvement in existing and new markets.

Dynamic Competence

The combined influence of changing markets, technology, or organizational behavior often results in an existing competence rendered less capable of supporting ongoing financial performance. Teece, Pisano, and Shuen (1997) emphasized the key role of managers is that of leading actions that result in adapting, integrating, and reshaping organizational skills, resources, and competences. The authors use the term "dynamic capabilities" to describe this managerial capability. A dynamic orientation requires the capacity to learn and adapt when confronted with new situations or market conditions. O'Driscoll, Carson, and Gilmore (2001) proposed that a failure to reconcile existing competences and acquire new competences may eventually lead a firm into to a "competence trap." This occurs because the organization has failed to recognize that changes in market conditions, technology, or behavior of competition have occurred. As a consequence, the organization remains fixated upon exploiting competences that no longer provide the basis for sustaining competitive advantage. O'Driscoll, Carson, and Gilmore posited avoidance of the competence trap involves engaging in new knowledge acquisition. This permits recognition of new entrepreneurial opportunities and an assessment of whether exploitation of new ideas will require utilization of existing or totally new competences.

Kuratko, Montagno, and Hornsby (1990) concluded that senior management's willingness to facilitate, promote, champion, and support entrepreneurial behavior with the allocation of adequate resources to support innovation is critical. They opined that senior management's vision must ensure all employees understand and accept that innovation is the organization's fundamental long-term strategy for optimizing future performance. This perspective can be expanded to include senior managers' willingness to provide entrepreneurial staff with autonomy, delegated authority to make decisions, freedom from excessive supervision, and removal of restrictive controls over access to needed resources.

Birkinshaw and Gibson (2004) noted that differences can arise between existing and new entrepreneurial strategies. They proposed that firms' internal environment must be "ambidextrous." This is necessary to enable a firm to switch between explorative and exploitative learning to enable the firm to handle contradictions that exist between current mainstream activities and future more entrepreneurial actions. To ensure the success of organizational ambidexterity, senior managers must present entrepreneurship as the "dominant logic" within the organization.

Playbook Guideline 49: Technological entrepreneurial outcomes are enhanced when the internal organizational environment is ambidextrous

Competence Enhancement

Innovation can range from incremental improvements through to radical change of an entrepreneurial nature leading to fundamental market change or the creation of totally new markets. The complex nature of many radical innovations means that many firms lack the resources and competences to effectively manage all aspects of the required entrepreneurial activities. As a consequence, there is often the need for organizations to engage in interorganizational collaboration and to become members of innovation networks (Pyka 2002).

Colarelli, O'Connor, and DeMartino (2006) identified three competences that capture the requirements for success in radical innovation. These are discovery, incubation, and acceleration. Discovery includes all activities that create, recognize, elaborate, and articulate opportunities. Key skills for this competency are in exploration and conceptualization in the areas of technical discovery and market evaluation to identify opportunities. Incubation involves radical opportunities to evolve into viable business propositions. Acceleration includes those activities that permit the developed idea to evolve into a revenue-generating proposition. However, it is increasingly unlikely that organizations own all of the necessary competences to engage in radical innovation. Hence, in today's technologically complex business environments, entrepreneurial success will often be critically influenced by the way firms collaborate with other organizations and participate in networks to access the competences that are lacking inside their own operation.

Collaboration can also be important in the acquisition of new knowledge, which can enhance innovation and entrepreneurial activities. In most industries, the key source of this new knowledge is through interaction with other supply chain members. Whether this new knowledge has any impact on existing competences will be determined by whether the firm has cutting-edge capabilities in relation to innovation management. Firms with a high knowledge reception capability are able to gain more information on products, technical issues, the market, and customer needs. Companies with high knowledge reception, therefore, are more able to convert knowledge into understanding that can enhance their entrepreneurial innovation capabilities (Lin, Wang, and Kung 2015).

Playbook Guideline 50: Technological entrepreneurial outcomes can be enhanced through interorganizational collaboration

Disruptive Technology

Case Aims: To illustrate how a new technology can obsolete the existing competences among incumbent firms

Technological entrepreneurship often relies on the exploitation of a totally new or emerging scientific or technological development, which results in a technical discontinuity within an industrial sector. This type of discontinuity creates the potential problem for long-established incumbent firms of whether they have the necessary technological competences to respond to this form of competitive threat.

In their research on technical discontinuity, Rothaermel and Hill (2005) presented the following case materials of events in the computer industry, steel industry, pharmaceutical industry, and telecommunications industry:

(1)   *The Computer Industry*
Before 1981, the computer industry was dominated by vertically integrated enterprises. These firms manufactured most of the important components in the computer hardware systems, bundled the hardware components with proprietary operating system software and applications software, and sold them via their own sales forces. By virtue of its design, the PC signaled a transition from the closed-system architecture to open-system architecture and desktop computing. In the turbulence that followed, large numbers of new enterprises entered at every stage of the value chain as the industry de-integrated. The center of gravity in the industry shifted rapidly away from incumbent enterprises, such as DEC, Wang, Unisys, and IBM, toward new entrants, such as Compaq, Intel, and Microsoft. The arrival of networking based on client server architecture in the late 1980s and the Internet in the 1990s further accelerated this shift. The emergence of these new players devalued the upstream R&D and production assets

of incumbent enterprises, which had little relevance to emerging PC firms such as Apple, Compaq, and Dell. Following the lead set by pioneers, new entrants were able to build computers using off-the-shelf modular components and simple manufacturing processes. The closed-system design philosophy and technical competences of the incumbents was contrary to the mindset required to produce low-cost, open-system personal computers.

(2)   *The Steel Industry*

The electric arc furnace was invented in the 1930s, but the technology did not become commercially viable until the late 1960s, when it became the basis for creating the first mini-mills. One of the pioneering mini-mill companies, Nucor, began operating its first mini-mill in 1969, but it took several more years to develop the technology to a level of cost-effectiveness that would provide a competitive advantage over the large traditional steel firms whose operations involved the use of coke ovens and blast furnaces.

(3)   *The Pharmaceutical Industry.*

Many human illnesses are caused by the body's overproduction or underproduction of certain proteins. Scientific understanding of the role of recombinant DNA in this process has major implications for introduction of new technologies into the pharmaceutical industry. It was new entrants who were the first to develop this potentially powerful new technology. The first biotechnology drug, Humulin, a genetically engineered human insulin, reached the market in 1982. The commercialization of Humulin was based on an alliance between the biotechnology start-up Genentech, which discovered and developed the new drug, and the established pharmaceutical company Eli Lilly, which managed the drug through clinical trials and government approval.

Biotechnology represents a radically different paradigm for discovering and developing new drugs with the skill loss for a scientist making the transition from the traditional drug screening paradigm to that of genetic engineering estimated to exceed 80 percent (Rothaermel 2001). However, biotechnology does not alter the regulatory process imposed by governments and requires the same schedule of clinical trials. Competence in testing and gaining approval meant that the incumbent drug firms were able to enter into alliances with these new start-ups, thereby causing the former to remain in business, despite the emergence of this technological discontinuity.

Creativity

Entrepreneurship can be considered as a process involving the identification and exploitation of opportunities that have not been previously considered. The activity of being entrepreneurial will involve individuals perceiving a potential opportunity on the basis of their information, knowledge, and experience.

As summarized in Table 6.1, three styles of decision making have been identified in the entrepreneurship literature (Cunhae 2007). The rational perspective involves consideration of factors such as risk-taking propensity, available information, and available options. The alternative approach of intuition may possibly be a distinguishing characteristic of many successful entrepreneurs. Improvisation may play an important role in the venture-creation process because due to the unstructured nature of opportunities, entrepreneurs need to deal with problems as they emerge and craft solutions on the spur of the moment. In such situations, they

Table 6.1 Three modes of entrepreneurial decision making*

	Rational	Intuitive	Improvisational
Logic	Science	Art	Craft
Process	1. Define 2. Diagnose 3. Design 4. Decide	Prepare Incubate Illuminate Verify	Enact Select Retain
The entrepreneurial information source	Facts	Ideas	Experiences
The mental process	Planning and programming	Visioning and imagining	Venturing and learning
Operational environment	Clear issues Reliable data Structured world	Ideas Commitment	Time pressures Confusing situations

Source: * Modified from Mintzberg and Westley 2001.

cannot make use of detailed and elaborated plans. On the contrary, they have to make decisions in real time, making do with whatever resources are currently available. In terms of the most appropriate decision-making style likely to result in the most successful outcomes, it is possibly best to assume that a contingency situation exists, which means entrepreneurs may utilize different styles depending on the situation that they are currently facing.

Companies seeking to engage in entrepreneurship are reliant on individual employee capabilities, not just in relation to their technological competence, but also in regard to creativity. The early stages of entrepreneurial activity have been identified as phases of opportunity identification, planning, and marshalling of resources (McGee et al. 2009). Given that uncertainty plays an important role in innovation entrepreneurial new product development processes, individuals and organizations are often required to rely on creativity to deal with the existence of uncertainty.

Blauth, Mauer, and Brettel (2014) proposed that employees engaged in being creative face a series of challenges. First, employees have to overcome uncertainty in perceiving opportunities that they decide to transform into real business. Second, they have to overcome uncertainty in knowing how to go about their project. Third, uncertainty arises from their corporate environment in which they decide to leverage an opportunity, but may a face a potential mismatch between required and available resources. These factors infer that entrepreneurial decision making will often rely on effectuation. Sarasvathy (2001) considered that this process is heavily reliant on creativity because opportunities are created, rather than based on detailed available information.

Effectuation consists of four dimensions that are contrasted with causation-based decision making. These are (i) the starting point for venturing, (ii) the attitude toward risk, (iii) the approach toward stakeholders, and (iv) the association with contingencies. Effectuators start with available means instead of using a goal orientation, invest what they can afford to lose instead of trying to predict expected returns, rely on partnerships rather than execute competitive analysis, and embrace rather than avoid unexpected events.

Individuals engaged in causation-based decision making deal with uncertainty through believing they "know better." Although this is a valid decision logic in situations of low to moderate uncertainty, it becomes a futile endeavor in unknowable contexts. Hence, Blauth, Mauer, and Brettel (2014) posited that in relation to creativity, it can be expected that the time invested in "knowing better" comes at the cost of practiced creativity. This can be contrasted with effectuation, which is more about implementing actions, despite the level of uncertainty.

In the case of incremental new product development, the standard approach is to define a goal and plan the steps in accordance with using predefined strategies and market-driven objectives. In contrast, the effectual approach usually starts with an assessment of available means, which are the resources that are available in the current situation. These resources include personal knowledge, experience, and resources provided by the company, such as financial support or the support of senior management. The way available resources are perceived and how to exploit them is crucial as individuals seek alternative, efficient ways of exploiting these existing resources. Furthermore, the scale of creativity may result from combining together what others might perceive as unrelated resources (Sternberg and Lubart 1997).

Playbook Guideline 51: Successful technological entrepreneurial outcomes are often reliant on creativity

Idea Generation

Case Aims: To describe the idea generation behavior exhibited by technological entrepreneurs

Entrepreneurs have a base of domain knowledge essential to performing creative transformational processes that lead to creative generation of new ideas (Shane 2000). Knowledge is a key to creative entrepreneurial actions, such as opportunity recognition and knowledge asymmetry; this can result in different entrepreneurs in the same environment coming up with radically different ideas. To gain further understanding of the implications of this outcome in terms of the ideation process exhibited by entrepreneurs, Gemmell, Boland, and Kolb

(2011) interviewed founders and/or senior executives in a number of American technology start-up businesses.

The researchers concluded that technology entrepreneurs utilize a variety of behaviors, techniques, and thought processes to develop, refine, and validate creative ideas, as well as filtering them based on perceived usefulness. Three key ideation processes identified included (i) utilization of complex and sophisticated social networks as sources of ideas and to test, refine, and validate trial ideas, (ii) exhibiting domain specificity by filtering ideas outside specific markets and technologies, and (iii) actively experimenting with ideas rather, than engage in protracted conceptual analysis.

CHAPTER 7

Strategizing

The Strategy Paradox

The importance of risk management, the exploitation of available information, and providing employees with clear guidance on the relationship between their role and overall aims of an organization means most firms establish a clearly defined, formalized strategy to guide their operations. The purpose of the strategy is to define the benefit that provides the basis for the competitive advantage through which to achieve specified performance. Strategy implementation is achieved through utilization of an appropriate marketing and internal value-added activities (Chaston 2013).

The use of strategy in the real world is evidenced by the fact that, in many major consumer goods companies, annual plans are guided by the overall strategy that is deemed most capable of supporting a positioning that will ensure achievement of forecasted performance (Mahdi et al. 2015). Although there is no reason to doubt the benefits that a strategy may confer, some researchers, especially those examining the behavior of entrepreneurial organizations, have identified cases where an organization is performing well, but there is no evidence that activities are being guided by a clearly defined strategy. Furthermore, materials concerning the activities of entrepreneurs such as Larry Page and Sergey Brin during the development of the technology that provided the basis for launching Google, or Chad Hurley, Steve Chen, and Jawed Karim's creation of the online video streaming proposition YouTube, evidence the primary focus of such individuals was about validating the technical feasibility of their idea, without any attempt to define a marketing strategy to guide their development activities (Chaston 2016).

Mintzberg's (1990) explanation for the lack of strategy during the development of an entrepreneurial proposition was that where a marketing strategy exists, this has evolved gradually over time, as individuals acquire a deeper understanding of the factors influencing success. Mintzberg's

(1999) typology for this type of strategic behavior is this is reflective of a "Learning School" approach to organizational management. In his view, the conventional linear sequential planning approach, which he described as the "Design School," involves the specification of a deliberate, detailed strategy, which, in his opinion, no longer remains feasible in today's increasingly uncertain world.

In commenting on the relationship between the existence of clearly defined strategy and firm performance, Dess, Lumpkin, and Covin (1997) posited this depended on factors such as a firm's competitive environment, organizational structure, position of the product of the product life cycle (PLC) curve, and speed or magnitude of technological change. Support for this perspective is provided by Covin and Slevin (1990), who empirically determined that in a hostile, rapidly changing, or heterogeneous market environment, higher financial performance was achieved by firms that had avoided being locked into utilizing a clearly articulated strategy to the define nature of the marketing process.

Playbook Guideline 52: Technological entrepreneurial successes are rarely the outcome of a carefully crafted long-term organizational strategy

Strategy-As-Practice

The traditional perspective on strategic planning is this is a formal, process-based activity involving an examination of the external environment and internal capabilities. An alternative model is that based on organizations developing and reining their strategies incrementally in the light of new information and opportunities. Research to generate understanding of this later model has involved redirecting the research away from the strategy process to focus on strategy-as-practice (S-as-P). This latter orientation emphasis is concerned with the tacit knowledge of how things work as opposed to the explicit knowledge of formal strategic planning models (Whittington 2003).

Jarrat and Stiles (2010) opined that in the context of S-as-P there is an interaction between the strategist, the organization's collective structures, and the activity of strategizing (Figure 7.1). The strategist, who often is the founder in a small firm and a member of the senior management team

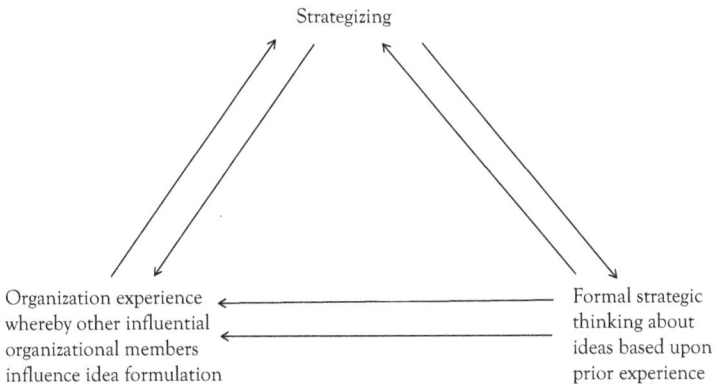

Figure 7.1 The strategising process

Source: Modified from Jarret and Stiles 2010.

in larger organizations, draws upon their own experience and frames of reference to evolve an appropriate strategic philosophy. Their position in the organization and allocated responsibility for strategy determination means their strategizing is likely to be highly influential within their organization. The degree to which their ideas are accepted will depend on the nature and outcome of interaction with others within the organization, whose own views are reflective of prior experience and involvement in learning.

Jarrat and Stiles concluded that the views and decisions of the strategist are influenced by their perspective on matters such as environmental stability, intensity of competition, and their organization's internal capabilities. Where the strategist is confident that the future will be similar to the past, the tendency is to rely upon structured, analytical models to validate the selected future with the outcome often being little alteration in the organization's business plans. In those cases where the future is perceived as dynamic and complex, such as that to be expected for an organization engaged in technological entrepreneurship, the strategizing process will usually involve the strategist in reflective thinking about a wide range of possible scenarios. These are then widely discussed within the organization before any final decision is reached. The researchers further concluded that where the future is perceived as dynamic and complex, the strategist will accept that traditional methodologies and planning tools are unable to capture and permit analysis of the current and emerging environment.

A key factor influencing strategy is market understanding. Where an entrepreneur is engaged in idea generation at the early stages of a radical innovation, there is likely to be little or no information available on the nature of the market into which the new proposition is to be launched. Under these circumstances, the entrepreneur is forced to rely upon intuition to guide the development process, based on their own internal mental map of how their idea can be converted into a viable commercial proposition (Chaston and Sadler-Smith 2012). Once the new proposition has evolved into a tangible entity and introduced to the market, this activity will generate new information that begins to enhance the entrepreneur's understanding of issues such as customer need, potential revenue, and reaction of competition. Over time, the depth and degree of understanding will continue to increase, and this can be expected to be accompanied by the emergence of a more well-defined strategy for guiding the marketing process.

Playbook Guideline 53: In the case where minimal market information is available, technological entrepreneurs will tend to rely upon intuition

Emergent Strategy

Covin, Green, and Slevin (2006) opined that entrepreneurial strategies are more likely to be emergent (i.e., realized patterns of actions not explicitly intended) than deliberate. As illustrated in Figure 7.2, identified uncertainty in relation to markets and new technology is a crucial constituent that influences the strategy-making process (Elbanna and Child 2007). Chari et al. (2014) identified two important dimensions of uncertainty, namely market dynamism reflected in rate of market change and technological instability over time.

Emergent strategies will evolve over time, reflecting the influence of organizational learning that occurs as new knowledge is acquired about markets and ongoing development of new technology. Feedback from the market and internally in relation to organizational processes will cause managers to reconsider and fine-tune the scope of their marketing strategies. The consequence of information changing managerial thinking means realized strategies do not often correspond with the initially

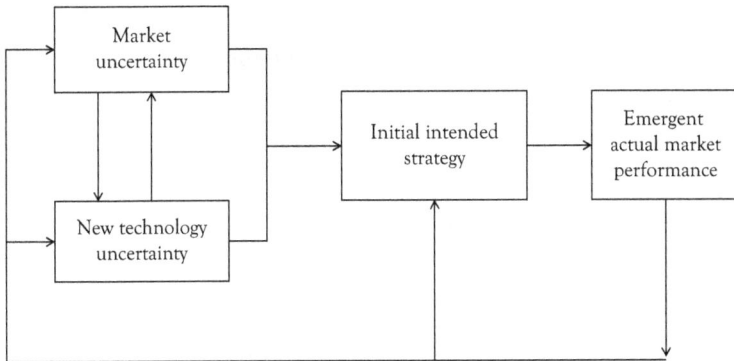

Figure 7.2 Emergent strategy development and revision

projected plans. Furthermore, some strategies may remain unrealized, having been proved unfeasible and needing to abandoned (Patrizi et al. 2013).

Playbook Guideline 54: Where technological entrepreneurial strategies exist, these will usually have evolved over time on the basis of organizational learning

Market Learning

In those cases where the entrepreneur is totally focused on proving the technical viability of their idea, the situation may exist where there is no understanding of potential market opportunity. Hence, this knowledge will only arise once the new product or service is launched, at which point, preliminary answers are generated to the key questions of (i) Who is the customer?, (ii) What benefit do customers seek?, (iii) How does a customer become aware of the new goods?, and (iv) Through which channel is the item purchased?

It is unlikely that a large existing firm would wait until market launch before seeking some understanding of the market opportunity. This is because the senior management recognizes that the potential risks associated with developing a new technology demand some form of market assessment prior to approving any major investment to progress a new entrepreneurial idea. Some firms will tend to rely upon utilization of the "stage gate" model where an assessment occurs as a sequential process constituted of the seven components of idea generation, idea screening, concept development, business planning, prototype development, test marketing, and market launch (Cooper, Edgett, and Kleinschmidt 1997).

In their evaluation of the benefits of utilizing the stage gate model in the case of entrepreneurial products, Millier and Palmer (2001) noted the model involves making certain critical assumptions. These are that the product can be characterized as having features or benefits, which potential customers can understand, and that the market for such a product is readily identifiable. They opined that successful determination of market opportunity is the lowest when firms are engaged in seeking to determine market opportunity for technology-based, new-to-the-world ideas. This is because the newness of the technology means that respondents to conventional market research activities, such as interviews or surveys, will have minimal understanding of the nature or benefits of the proposition being described. Under these circumstances, the large firm may have to rely upon internal opinions, external experts, or other members of the supply chain to offer judgment-based opinions, which may or may not be correct (Evans and Johnson 2013).

Playbook Guideline 55: Understanding of actual opportunity for a radical entrepreneurial idea often can only be achieved by gaining experience from an initial market launch

Strategy Validation

Validation of a technology-based entrepreneurial (TE) strategy is often associated with organizations further evolving their strategizing through either market success or failure. It is not unusual for the selected TE strategy to require changes in the pattern of decision making within the organization. In some cases, the new strategy demands the creation of a radically different organization.

A key objective of the TE strategy is to achieve a close fit between organization and the prevailing market environment. Where achievement of fit is deemed unlikely, then the TE strategy may require the organization moving to a new market environment more conducive to sustaining future performance. Although entrepreneurial behavior is usually presented in the literature as a proactive process, the antecedents may be rooted in a reactive response to an adverse situation, such a sudden deterioration in financial performance. In this latter scenario, the aim of moving to a TE strategy is to support a "turnaround" in order to sustain long-term organizational viability (Piercy, Cravens, and Lane 2010).

Lumpkin and Dess (1996) suggested the dimensions that usually constitute a TE strategy; they are an entrepreneurial orientation, innovativeness, risk taking, proactiveness, and competitive aggressiveness. Dess et al. expressed a similar view, positing that evolving a TE strategy represents a distinctive process that is characterized by experimentation, innovativeness, risk taking, and proactive assertiveness. In order to construct an effective TE strategy, the organization will need to assess the potential impact of the three key variables, namely market opportunity, viable technology, and internal capability.

In the case of consumer branded products, such as detergents or coffee, the low-tech nature of these goods means radical entrepreneurial innovation is rarely feasible (Chaston 2016). As a consequence, associated marketing conventions will remain unchanged for many years. This situation causes companies to focus on the use of conventional strategies and processes to defend their market position. In theory, such firms could consider other forms of entrepreneurial activity in relation to their marketing mix or organizational processes.

A very different scenario, however, is faced by companies operating in high-tech sectors such as information technology (IT) or electronic communications. This is because the rapidity with which new technological advances occur means that to survive, organizations must be capable of responding to the reality that existing conventions are difficult to sustain over the longer term. As a consequence, technological advances often result in existing industry conventions being broken.

In relation to the TE strategy, both exploration and exploitation have emerged as the twin concepts in relation to determining competitive advantage and organizational survival (Gupta Smith and Shalley 2006). Kollmann and Stöckmann (2014) posited that most firms would implicitly favor exploration because this permits swift movement toward identifying new opportunities. This attitude is especially prevalent in volatile markets because of the risks associated with allocating scarce resources to any exploitation of any of the identified potential opportunities. Exploration and exploitation are not mutually exclusive activities because very successful companies are likely to pursue both types of activities. Nevertheless, as demonstrated in Table 7.1, the two approaches exhibit very different attributes.

Firms engaging in exploratory innovation may obtain positive performance outcomes, such as discovering new competences, and products that can shape the rules of competition in ways that rivals will find difficult to imitate, thereby leading to unique selling propositions and enhanced customer satisfaction. Firms that shun exploration risk can become vulnerable to the effects of obsolescence because their continued involvement in saturated markets may lead to diminishing financial return. Exploitative innovation is also essential because firms that ignore this activity may run the risks of expending funds on experimentation, without gaining any real benefits. Hence, exploitation is necessary in order to realize positive returns on investments in entrepreneurial innovation through outcomes such as increased efficiency, cost reduction, and superior delivery of customer needs.

Entrepreneurial innovation can facilitate differentiation from competitors. Differentiation can be achieved by exploration through developing

Table 7.1 Innovation typology and attributes*

Exploitative innovation	Explorative innovation
• Incremental change	• Radical or disruptive change
• Incremental innovation	• Radical or disruptive innovation
• Existing business	• Future or emerging business
• Short-run perspective	• Long-run perspective
• Operational focus	• Strategic focus
• Existing technologies	• New technologies
• Certainties	• Uncertainties
• Efficiency	• Adaptability
• Mechanic structures	• Organic structures
• Conventional	• Entrepreneurial
• Stability	• Change
• Sustaining advantages	• New advantages
• Convergent behavior	• Divergent behavior

Source: * Modified from Simsek et al. 2009.

creative new offerings to satisfy customer needs. Exploitative innovations such as efficiency improvements or cost reduction can facilitate negation of competitor offerings based on superior value claims. The risk with an organizational focus on internal stability that originates from past success may lead to structural and cultural inertia. This can be an obstacle to change when there is a major shift in environmental conditions (O'Reilly and Tushman 2011). In rapidly changing environments, avoiding organizational inertia is of utmost importance because past organizational strengths can become future liabilities (Danes 2013.

Ambidexterity involves the dual management of seemingly opposing tasks, which involves the ability to switch to different operational modes when pursuing entrepreneurial innovation. Successful ambidextrous organizations are able to integrate exploitative and explorative activities with the aim of excelling in the present and in the future. Examples of large existing corporations that have been successful in building an ambidextrous capability include GlaxoSmithKline Seiko, Hewlett-Packard, and Johnson and Johnson (O'Reilly and Tushman 2011).

Ambidextrous innovation management is often necessary because the organization faces two forms of environmental changes, namely environments evolving incrementally requiring a need for efficiency enhancement and discontinuous changes demanding radical innovation. The latter is usually mandatory in high-tech industry sectors where there are very short PLCs. This situation caused Kollman et al. to posit that entrepreneurial companies in innovative industries are more likely to manage growth ambidextrously than entrepreneurial companies in low-tech industries.

Ambidextrous organizations require a senior management orientated toward supporting both exploitative and explorative activities. O'Reilly and Tushman noted that some organizations, although aiming explicitly at the attainment of both goals, face the danger of failing because of an inability "to play two games simultaneously." Entrepreneurial activities need to be organized by building loose and adaptive organic structures with a culture that emphasizes risk-taking, speed, flexibility, and experimentation. In relation to achieving a balance between different activities, structural ambidexterity ensures effective operation of exploitative and explorative tasks by organizing these into different innovation streams. Interaction between all areas of the organization is important to sustain

Change in product/service benefit(s)

Totally new benefit proposition

Value innovation	Radical innovation

Market convention status

← Unchanged convention(s) ————————————— Totally new convention(s) →

New improved innovation	Disruptive innovation

Completely unchanged benefit proposition

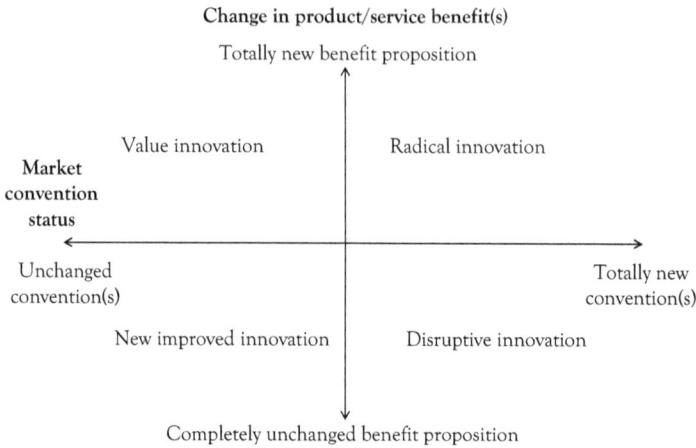

Figure 7.3 Alterative innovation propositions

knowledge flows and to permit everybody to understand what activities are occurring elsewhere within the organization. It is vital that those engaged in radical innovation do not encounter internal organizational resistance from the more conventionally orientated areas of the operation.

One approach to determining the degree of entrepreneurial innovation associated with the observed strategies of organizations is to classify outcomes in relation to the dimensions of (i) scale of breaking with existing market conventions and (ii) the degree to which the benefit proposition has been changed. As summarized in Figure 7.3, this taxonomy generates four possible outcomes.

As new entrepreneurial ventures gain understanding from their experience of market conditions, this can lead to recognition of the need to review issues such as the viability of the selected competitive advantage and the distinctive competences required to sustain ongoing success. As summarized in Figure 7.4, these interactions may result in the identification of an optimal future strategy too. Essentially, what will often occur is a reallocation of internal resources to achieve closer alignment with the aim of creating a sustainable competition advantage. This process has been described by Teece (2007) as permitting (i) sensing and shaping opportunities and threats, (ii) seizing opportunities, and (iii) maintaining competitiveness through enhancing, combining, protecting, and, when necessary, reconfiguring the business enterprises' intangible and tangible assets.

This need for re-evaluation and reconsideration of the emergent strategy has been described by Burgelman and Siegel (2008) as the "stretching

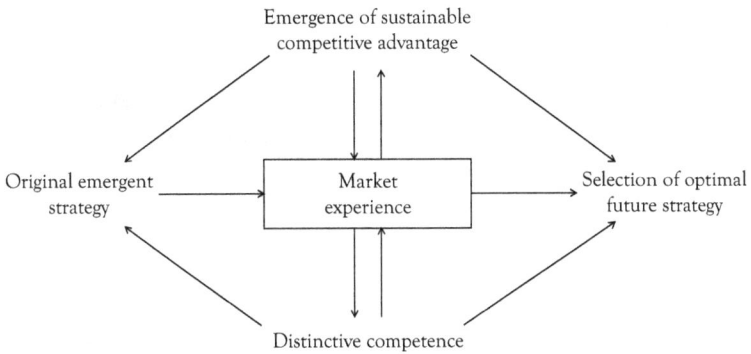

Figure 7.4 Strategy re-alignment

of the rubber bands." This term reflects the fact that proposing a change can be the cause strategic dissonance between senior management and the employees, where is the need to revise assigned roles and development projects. To gain further understanding of the issues associated with rubber band stretching, Burgelman and Siegel took a case-based analysis of the activities of a number of American high-tech ventures. Their research revealed that while well-managed established companies, such as Intel and GE, have developed a disciplined strategy-making process that can accommodate changes caused by gaining market experience, new high-tech ventures often do not immediately adopt such processes. This is because, during the early days of the venture, the primary focus is on proving the feasibility of a new technology and/or the viability of a new product. As a consequence, these latter organizations often have benefited from earlier understanding of the strategic implications of their core technological invention in relation to both strengths and potential weaknesses.

> *Playbook Guideline 56: Long-term technological entrepreneurial success is usually dependent on involvement in both explorative and exploitative innovation*

Business Models

The complexity of many markets and the risks associated with developing and launching a product based on exploitation of entirely new technology has, in recent years, led to the emergence of the concept that to reduce risks, as part of the emergent strategy development process, organizations should create a business model to define all of the variables associated with managing a market system. Morris, Schindehutte, and Allen (2005) proposed that *a business model is a concise representation of how an inter-related set of decision variables in the areas of venture strategy, architecture, and economics are addressed to create sustainable competitive advantage in defined markets.*

Definition of an appropriate business model can assist in identifying key factors such as the value proposition, target market, revenue model, partner network, internal infrastructure, and processes. By rethinking and reconfiguring these elements, the technological entrepreneur may be able to identify a new approach that can provide the basis for a new model that confers a competitive advantage. An effective illustration of this approach is provided by Jeff Bezos who sought to exploit the Internet and used the technology to create the highly successful online retail venture, Amazon.

Chesbrough (2010) opined business model development as being a constant experimentation and adjustments to changing market environments. Schoen et al. (2005) proposed the process of business model development as a transitional phase between the invention and the innovation stage, thereby implying that the process of business model development for the commercialization of innovations is a fundamental aspect within the innovation process. Dmitriev et al. (2014) undertook a case-based study of three technological start-ups and one technological spin-off. Despite the nature of the technological innovation across the four firms being unique and highly context-dependent, the researchers noted similar processes of interactions and cycles in business model development within all four firms. The process of business model development appeared as a cyclical, continuous process of conceptualizing value through the activities of market segmentation, value proposition, and the revenue modeling, and organizing for value creation involving cost and revenue estimation, finding equipment, resources and partners to permit collaborative innovation.

Playbook Guideline 57: Development and utilization of a new business model can enhance the chances of achieving technological entrepreneurial success

CHAPTER 8

Managing Process

Managerial Dilemma

The key managerial issue facing a small technology start-up is usually that of ensuring access to resources, especially financial, as the project progresses from idea generation through to successful market launch (Chaston 2014). In large organizations, resource acquisition is a relatively unimportant matter. Instead the primary focus is on achieving an equitable balance between sustaining ongoing operations while concurrently providing adequate support for entrepreneurial activities. Sharma (1999) posited that this balancing act resulted in large firms facing the following dilemmas:

1. Managing all of the available ideas
2. Ensuring younger managerial staff has the capability to make commercially viable decisions
3. Justifying the allocation of staff during the development phase when no revenue is being generated
4. Ensuring an equitable balance of resources across the organization
5. Defining a launch strategy that is financially sustainable

Playbook Guideline 58: Careful management is required in order to achieve an appropriate balance between existing activities and involvement in radical innovation

Regaining Creativity

Case Aims: To demonstrate that excessively structured management systems can have an adverse impact on leading-edge innovations

Founded in 1902, the American 3M Corporation established a reputation for outstanding innovation. However, in the late 1990s, 3M experienced declining performance, probably reflecting that it had become too big and risk-adverse (Radjou, Prabhu, and Ahuja 2012). 3M hired Jim McNerney as the new CEO. Having previously worked at GE, he brought with him a disciplined attitude aimed creating a more efficient organization to be achieved through the use of the Six Sigma management philosophy. This highly structured system emphasizes predictability and certainty and is considered to have contributed to significantly improving profitability.

When Six Sigma techniques were utilized in 3M's R&D laboratories, the aim was to systematize and standardize the cause innovation processes to be faster and more cost-effective. Innovators responded to the new philosophy by focusing on improving existing products and avoided involvement in high-risk leading-edge research. By 2005, 3M's revenue from new products had fallen from the traditional 30 percent to only 21 percent of the total sales. McNerney's replacement George Buckley perceiving the negative aspects of the Six Sigma process began to de-emphasize the concept within the organization. One important move was to reinstate the 15 percent rule self-directed projects concept, which gave 3M innovators the flexibility and freedom to pursue radical ideas without the fear of censure by senior management.

Leadership

R&D groups tend to differ from other teams within organizations because of the time-lagged, sporadic nature their outputs (Narayanan 2001). Innovation tasks usually involve a high risk of failure and frequently experience disruptions, delays, and setbacks (Kim, Min, and Cha 1999). All of these properties pose unique challenges for team leaders. Certain leadership practices have been identified as facilitative of individual creativity and team innovativeness. These include consultative leadership, commitment, charisma, work-related rather than administrative communications, high levels of information sharing, support for new ideas, focus on interpersonal skills of members, and a commitment to learning (Stoker et al. 2001).

Zhenga, Khoury, and Grobmeiera (2010) undertook a study of four technology teams to gain further understanding of the leadership role in R&D environments. The four teams demonstrated similar leadership characteristics as well as differences. The researchers concluded that the team leaders all exhibited the following common traits:

1. Simultaneously focused on the internal and external domains of the team
2. Steering rather than channeling efforts
3. A hands-off style and exerting minimum oversight
4. Buffering by serving as the team gatekeeper
5. Acting as the primary communications channel
6. Rainmaking by promoting their team inside and outside the organization

Playbook Guideline 59: The effectiveness of team leaders is critically important in ensuring the success of technological entrepreneurship endeavors

Managing Teams

Managerial leadership style and work environment significantly influence innovative performance, especially in the case of self-directed work teams (DiBella 1995). Thamhain's (2003) study of R&D teams revealed certain metrics commonly used by team leaders and managers as indicators of innovative performance included (i) the number of new products or services introduced to market, (ii) time-to-market, (iii) cost and performance improvements, and (iv) number of generated patents. For teams and individuals, meaningful performance measures were more difficult to define.

Thamhain opined that one of the major challenges in innovation management is to achieve the involvement of the entire workforce. This is because high-tech innovation is a multidisciplinary effort, involving teams of people and support organizations interacting in a highly complex, intricate, and sometimes, even chaotic way. Factors of influence for achieving convergence between individual and overall organizational goals include effective communication, information sharing, and integration of activities with a common focus on desired outcomes.

Dynamic Capability

Firms can reduce variability and create greater efficiency by developing and improving internal processes. These routines are less effective when efforts require higher levels of innovation, such as creating new product categories, developing new technologies, or entering new markets (Cooper, Edgett, and Kleinschmidt 2004). When uncertainty is high, deterministic systems and procedures designed to bring order to a situation may vitiate the chaos necessary for successful innovation. Schreyogg and Kliesch-Eberl (2007) posited that the key capability for innovation to occur is the dynamic ability to learn and improvise. This will permit the firm to respond to the need for change, regardless of the environment.

Innovation requires a search for new information outside the existing knowledge base, often in areas unrelated to current operations. The process can be uncertain as well as only being of relevant to a particular context. As a consequence, there will be a requirement to engage in experimentation to cope with high variation and diversity (March 1991). There may be little clarity about how particular decisions lead to particular outcomes. This situation will, therefore, demand ad hoc problem-solving and iterative adaptation to unpredictable outcomes (Winter 2003).

The creation of dynamic capability requires the presence of specialist personnel. Certain characteristics may not distinguish entrepreneurs from more conservative employees in areas such as in-depth expertise, problem-solving ability, and communication skills. But, other skills tend to be unique to entrepreneurs. These include a tolerance for high risk and ambiguity and the ability to persist and sell innovative ideas (Day 1994). The organizational environment is also highly important in enabling innovation. Project teams need to be able to interact and exchange information with others to engage in the high level of problem solving and creative action necessary for innovation. Communications about new ideas is best fostered in strong personal relationships because innovation often requires close collaboration between those who do not typically work together. Hence, in their relational support role, managers can facilitate communication by promoting collective understanding and interpersonal trust among employees (Dess et al. 2003).

Playbook Guideline 60: The complexity of many technological entrepreneurship projects demands the development of dynamic capabilities within the organization

Managing Technological Diversity

Case Aims: To illustrate how a complex high-tech organization may seek to achieve structure and order within the innovation process

Boeing Corporation is a highly diversified company engaged in areas that include (i) commercial aircraft products and services (ii) defense products such as military aircraft and missiles, (iii) space products such as satellites and launch vehicles, and (iv) a growing array of advanced networked system products for both commercial and defense applications. This diversity of products and services relies upon the sustained exploitation of innovation across a widening array of technologies. An enterprise such as Boeing usually requires the existence of a framework for managing innovation across many areas in a manner that is focused and connected, but without hindering creativity. Hence, the company has sought to avoid a personality-driven approach to research management because this may result in a R&D portfolio based on preferences and hunches, rather than providing the basis for a systematic view of the whole company and its opportunities (Lind 2006).

Boeing Corporation has identified certain key objectives that underpin decisions concerning the current and future innovation portfolio. These include projects being required to be:

1. Highly collaborative, drawing many types of participants together in the innovation process
2. Systematic, applying systems engineering principles and process concepts
3. Lean enabling enterprise-level R&D to respond effectively and efficiently to Boeing business needs
4. Continuous, enabling management of the portfolio in response to changes in company needs and opportunities as they arise

5. Traceable, ensuring clear linkage of R&D efforts to business needs

6. Promote a high level of innovation, experimentation, and discovery

7. Enable longer-term R&D to be properly related to near-term R&D

8. Draw appropriately from external and global sources of R&D such as labs, universities, and other companies

9. Manage complexity in a fashion that enables participants to know what they need to know and when they need to know it, without being overwhelmed with details they do not need

10. Be simple and clear, allowing people to quickly see how they can contribute and collaborate with others

Strategic Planning

The conventional view is that strategic planning promotes a careful review of the different options in various business environments, which increases the number of new product development (NPD) projects and enhances firm performance (Moorman and Miner 1998). Strategic planning is formal process that utilizes explicit procedures to determine specific, long-range objectives, generate alternative strategies, requires adherence to the selected strategy upon plan implementation, and utilizes a structured system to monitor results. By clarifying competitive threats and opportunities, the process provides the basis for implementing actions designed to enhance firm performance. Planning can help speed up the NPD process by resolving organizational conflicts and providing a clear vision for future activities. Christensen (1997) argued that planning based on sound market research, followed by execution provides that provides justification for strategic management being an effective and efficient process.

Eisenhardt and Tabrizi (1995) articulated the idea that improvisation or an experiential approach that lacks formal planning may increase the number of NPD projects. This is because such activities motivate the impromptu acquisition and application of knowledge and intelligence, which may be tangential to norms, rules, and conventions. The implication associated with this latter perspective is strategic planning could represents an inertial force that decreases the number of NPD projects.

Song et al. (2011) opined three reasons to support the view that strategic planning decreases the number of NPD projects. First, formal strategic planning may provide irrelevant and incomplete NPD knowledge because it cannot accommodate unexpected outcomes or problems that occur during the NPD process. Second, a formal strategic planning process designed to govern and control NPD activities may prevent employees from being innovative. Third, by their very nature, innovative and entrepreneurial initiatives cannot be planned precisely in advance. Fourth, strategic planning may promote a culture of inertia and rigidity within which creative ideas for projects that are not part of organizational memory are often rejected.

An experiential approach that eschews formal planning and focuses on improvisation can accelerate the ideation process. In addition, improvisation motivates the impromptu acquisition and application of knowledge, which helps teams generate more NPD projects by increasing the speed of the NPD activities. Additionally, a firm that emphasizes improvisation in NPD can continuously evaluate activities and outcomes. This will create more NPD projects than an organization that draws on resources from prior learning and strategies to respond to the changing market potential (Chelariu, Johnston, and Young 2002).

Playbook Guideline 61: Excessive reliance on formalized strategic planning can reduce the capabilities of the organization to identify and develop highly innovative new ideas

Radical Innovation

Rae (2007) noted that senior management behavior can adversely influence the functioning of an R&D project. Burgelman, Christensen, and Wheelwright (2008) found that the senior management within 3M's optical systems division did not differentiate between R&D projects. They used the same reporting structures and metrics to evaluate all their R&D projects, regardless of whether the project was incremental or radical. This resulted in project teams preferring more predictable projects with short-term rewards, which ultimately affected the long-term innovation performance at 3M.

Frameworks used to categorize R&D projects are usually based on the extent of change. Wheelwright and Clark (1992) used the product and process dimensions to evaluate the extent of change in project scope. They classified projects that have low levels of product and process change as "derivative projects," projects that have high levels of product and process change as "breakthrough projects," and projects with medium levels of product and process change as "platform projects."

R&D projects in high-tech organizations fall into three distinct categories based on their learning goals, namely radical innovation projects, incremental innovation projects, and hybrid projects. These three types of projects benefitted from different types of incentives, leadership, and team autonomy. Incremental innovation projects benefitted from outcome incentives, transactional leadership, and lower levels of team autonomy. In contrast, radical innovation projects benefitted from process incentives, transformational leadership, and higher levels of team autonomy. Transformational leaders are more able to promote risk taking and experimentation, which in turn encourages team members to search for novel solutions. Furthermore, these teams benefitted from higher levels of team autonomy because this permitted team members to adjust their assignments and goals. Hybrid projects will benefit from an ambidextrous leadership style and a reasonable level of team autonomy. Because these projects face pressures to find novel solutions under time or budget constraints, ambidextrous leadership promoted risk taking and experimentation, but also drove teams to meet explicit targets.

Playbook Guideline 62: Radical innovation can benefit from transformational leadership and high levels of team autonomy

Bootlegging

Case Aims: To illustrate how unofficial activities can enhance innovation within organizations

Bootlegging is an entrepreneurial process whereby employees seek to bypass corporate systems to engage in underground projects. For example, within BMW, the 12-cylinder engine was developed over a period of five years by a group of motor aficionados, without management approval. The engine was a success and contributed significantly to BMW's brand image of innovative automobile excellence (Anon 2006).

Augsdorfer (2008) posited bootleg entrepreneurs usually do not care whether bootlegging is permitted or not, or if the firm expects open communication about the activity. At Becton Dickinson, total transparency is perceived by senior management as an unrealistic demand and driven by wishful thinking. When managers know about bootleg projects, this will tend to cause questions to be asked, thereby reducing the researcher's sense of freedom. On the basis of available data, Augsdorfer proposed that the dilemmas faced by bootleggers include:

1. Creative people need an outlet for their creative energy and curiosity. Most formal organizations fail to provide sufficient space for people with ideas outside the mainstream.
2. Decisions that concern innovations are important, but often have to be taken under conditions of high technical and market uncertainty. They must be based on careful analysis, with uncertainties reduced to a minimum. Hence, the bootlegger may face a chicken-and-egg situation. Research is required to get the idea accepted. However, how does research commence without a go-ahead? The bootlegger must be willing to engage in unapproved informal research because it is unlikely that a formal approval will be given.
3. R&D budgets need to be planned. Usually, this happens annually when objectives are linked to budgets. But, great ideas often occur between planning periods.

These dilemmas can be overcome by resorting to underground activity. Serendipity, spin-offs from current research, or other unforeseen events are important in unleashing creative ideas. Dissatisfaction with a manager's decision or rising personal interest in a current topic is a further trigger. It is common to spend some hours bootlegging on a regular basis. Most bootleg projects were accepted by the firm after disclosure because they met the firm's business needs. Radical innovation depends on good ideas emerging from individual minds. Augsdorfer opined that bootleggers can be considered as creative because they think in a divergent way, opening up opportunities for the firm.

Augsdorfer also proposed that only occasionally do underground ideas create radical breakthroughs. Most companies interviewed characterized the usual bootleg idea as leading to a technological improvement. The technology of existing products is improved either by adding functionality or replacing technological imperfections with specific refinements.

Although bootleg entrepreneurs work outside any formal procedures, they are, in fact, controlled by friends, colleagues, and on occasion, by customers. Criticism by others is useful for distilling and refining the quality of the idea. Despite concerns senior management may have over their lack of control, bootlegging can provide an important catalyst for organizational creativity. This is because most outstanding new ideas typically emerge from a few creative individuals within an organization, who often question mainstream approaches. Hence, to ban or block bootlegging is likely to significantly reduce the innovative capabilities within an organization.

Playbook Guideline 63: Bootlegging can play an important role in stimulating creativity among the more entrepreneurial employees

CHAPTER 9

New Knowledge Acquisition

Knowledge

A key driving force influencing activities of entrepreneurs is the discovery and application of new knowledge that can provide the basis for innovation in existing industries and the creation of totally new industries. The issue facing senior managers is the degree to which their organization can rely on exploiting the existing knowledge versus new knowledge to support innovation. Existing knowledge tends to be widely available within an industrial sector, and hence, is rarely able to support any really radical, innovative ideas. As a consequence, entrepreneurial organizations have long understood the critical importance of sustaining their competence through the exploitation of new knowledge (Day and Schoemaker 2005).

Reliance upon the exploitation of existing knowledge will usually only permit the organization to sustain current business strategies, and in some cases, identify opportunities to utilize existing knowledge as the basis for product or market diversification. This does not mean, however, that organizations orientated toward implementing entrepreneurial strategies should ignore existing knowledge. In most cases, existing knowledge can provide a much lower risk source of future business revenue than is available from exploiting new knowledge. Hence, even entrepreneurial firms should seek to achieve an appropriate balance over the degree with which different sources of knowledge are to be utilized in relation to deciding about the involvement in low- versus high-risk propositions (Chaston 2004).

When new knowledge emerges, sometimes there may be no obvious immediate commercial applications. For example, when first invented, the laser was described as a "solution looking for a problem" (Shimizu 2010). The important issue in such cases is for the organization to permit a certain proportion of resources to be applied at looking for new application opportunities. One company that has excelled at applying this philosophy is 3M Corporation. Such was the case with the Post It note where a new glue formulation was developed, which exhibited poor adhesive properties. Subsequently, another 3M innovator sought just these qualities to develop a system for temporarily attaching a piece of paper to another surface without causing any damage to that surface (Garner 2005).

Entrepreneurs tend to be attracted to a leading-edge technology. This is important because this technology can provide the basis for above-average business performance through the creation of new products and new industries. In terms of analyzing future opportunities and threats, it is necessary to assess how new knowledge can be amplified by combining new knowledge with the current leading-edge technology. Organizations need to be aware that the interaction between new knowledge and a leading-edge core technology is a dynamic process (Chaston 2015). Firms engaged in the provision of professional services, such as accountancy practices, are continually seeking ways of replacing extremely expensive individual staff with machine-based solutions. This means an entrepreneurial organization must continually strive to identify and exploit new approaches for combining the latest advances in knowledge and IT to further enhance organizational performance.

Playbook Guideline 64: Successful technological entrepreneurship often relies upon combining different areas of leading-edge knowledge

Outsourcing

Case Aims: To illustrate the benefits of exploiting outsourcing elements of the innovation process to access new knowledge

Although lower transaction costs, such as lower wages, were initially a primary motivation in outsourcing, more recently, the concept has become recognized as an effective way of acquiring a wider breadth of new knowledge, thereby leveraging organizational assets for use in innovation. An example is provided by Apple's relationships with contract manufacturer Foxconn and a network of component suppliers, which permits a rapid rate of development for next-generation products.

Marion and Friar (2012) opined that firms engaged in successful innovation outsourcing should:

1. Select partners that complement and enhance their strategic mission
2. Exploit applied rapid prototyping solutions to support agile product development
3. Use short-run manufacturing partners to test market acceptance, rather than pushing toward costly and risky full commercialization at too early a stage in an innovation project
4. Take full advantage of outsourced partners to reduce fixed costs, add flexibility, and expand domain expertise

Accessing International Knowledge

Case Aims: To illustrate how firms are utilizing R&D centers to access overseas knowledge sources

Although the majority of high-tech firms still base the bulk of their R&D activities in their home country, in recent years, a number have begun to open new R&D centers overseas. Similar to outsourcing, the initial moves were usually motivated by a need to reduce operating costs. Over time, however, the more important reasons for the activity now include (Smallaski 1996):

1. The ability of the company to access new knowledge about relevant technology to suit overseas market circumstances.
2. Creating and international leveraging scientific and technical knowledge, some of which is tacit within a specific country.
3. Permitting organizations to separate routine and creative tasks or processes in order to distinguish predictable processes from nonpredictable ones.

Open Innovation

The traditional approach to innovation is this occurs inside the firm with no interaction with external sources. This "closed innovation" philosophy usually reflects management concerns over confidentiality and seeking to avoid pre-emptive actions by competition. In the face of increasing technological complexity and the need to optimize the acquisition of new knowledge, some organizations are engaging in "open innovation" involving collaboration with external parties (Chesbrough 2003).

Open innovation creates value by leveraging many more ideas from a variety of external sources and allows greater value capture in the utilization of the firm's existing assets. Lichtenthaler (2009) proposed open innovation is very useful when an organization is seeking to accelerate market acceptance for a new technology or new market standard. Lazzarotti, Manzini, and Pellegrini (2010) posited that, as firms increase their R&D activities, this will accompanied by more involvement in forming collaborative links with other organizations.

The risk facing firms is that a company relying too heavily on closed innovation may miss new market opportunities. This is because many new opportunities may fall outside of the organization's current business activities and technological competence or can only be exploited by working with other organizations. To avoid this outcome, the management needs to recognize that the boundary between a firm and the surrounding environment must be porous, thereby enabling the development of a collaborative approach to knowledge exploitation. Some high-tech firms are exploiting social media platforms to create open innovation approaches that can provide access a wider source of new knowledge and ideas. Known as "crowd sourcing," one of the leading players is the American corporation, Cisco (Ebner, Leimester, and Krcmar 2009).

Chesbrough and Crowther (2006) noted that low-tech and mature firms mainly use open innovation to in-source relevant knowledge and technologies, whereas outbound open innovation is far less widespread among these types of firms. Inbound sourcing methods include information transfer from informal networks, R&D collaboration, and technology acquisition. Simard and West (2006) distinguished between deep ties, which enable a firm to capitalize on existing knowledge and resources, and wide ties, which are more appropriate for locating new technological and market opportunities. Collaborations can have an explorative or exploitative purposes, and these will tend to be reflected in the type of actors in an innovation network.

Playbook Guideline 65: Technological entrepreneurship can often be assisted by engaging in open innovation

Networks

Modern technologies are often multitechnological in nature, demanding much higher levels of knowledge. This significantly complicates the innovation process (Narula 2004). Examples include industries such as automotive, aircraft, telecommunication, electrical equipment, computers, biotechnology, and new materials. Successful innovation usually requires a firm to complement their customer orientation with a distinct technology orientation that enables them to develop new solutions for already identified customer needs and to create forms of new customer demand. Narula posited that the multitechnological nature of complex innovation demands that, in addition to existing technological core competences, new complementary competences in other areas of science or technology are often required. However, due to the increased amount of knowledge required for complex innovations, these often have to be generated from many different sources. This usually requires access to a dense network of connections between institutions such universities, research institutes, suppliers, customers, and other partners. Exploitation of complementary competences within a network permits each organization to focus on optimization of the use of their respective core capabilities (De Liu, Gautam, and Andrew 2010).

Tell (2000) concluded that participation in innovation networks has several implications on the growth orientation of member companies. First, companies can expand their exploitation of the complementary knowledge of the partners in the network. Second, involvement allows a sharing of ideas by network partners such that, should an idea not fit with a company's strategy, other members of the network may progress the idea. Third, network membership can serve to broaden a firm's strategic perspective as a consequence access knowledge assets located in different organizations, which often have different innovation priorities and strategies. Ahuja, Galletta, and Carley (2000) defined network structure as existing in three dimensions, namely (i) the number of direct ties a focal actor has to partners, (ii) the number of indirect ties the actor has to the partners of other partners, and (iii) concerns about the ties between the focal actor's partners and the extent to which they are bound to one another.

Open innovation, therefore, cannot be regarded as the product of a single company, but as the product of interaction between two or more actors in a network. Technical solutions generated by one actor may be usable by another actor in another area. New ideas can, thus, be developed by combining the experience of various actors. Technological innovation often requires various forms of knowledge be combined or complimentary. Knowledge may be codified or noncodified. Less complex knowledge can usually be codified, whereas more complex knowledge often cannot. Noncodified knowledge is tacit knowledge such as know-how or unique experiences. Tacit knowledge can only be disseminated or transferred when the actors involved meet and interact (Rost 2011).

Playbook Guideline 66: The complexity of some technological entrepreneurship problems can only be overcome through participation in one or more networks

A Knowledge Network

Case Aims: To illustrate the role of knowledge networks in the production of innovative high-tech products

In the past, large companies have manufactured their own products, often using internally produced components. Such highly integrated companies created and captured a large share of the value of innovation, mostly in their home countries. Since then, supply chains in the global electronics industry have steadily disaggregated across corporate and national boundaries (Dedrick and Kraemer 2006).

This new structure represents an innovation and technology network in which the lead firm acts a knowledge hub linking together the various sources of technological knowledge and competences made available to and from other network members. For example, in the initial iPod models, there was little technology that was unique to Apple. With each new generation of iPod, new network members were recruited. The producers of high-value, critical components capture the largest share of the value of an innovative product. For the 30-GB Video iPod, the highest-value components are the hard drive and the display, both supplied by Japanese companies Toshiba and Toshiba-Matsushita, respectively. (Kinden, Kraemer, and Dedrick 2009).

Alliances

Acceleration of R&D efforts and the development of internal capabilities are no longer sufficient to cope with the increasing cost, speed, and complexity of developments in high-tech industries. Even the largest companies are obliged to access external sources of new knowledge through activities such as licensing, alliances, or mergers and acquisitions (M&As) (Babarinsa 2011). A major catalyst is increased global competition and advances in technology, which have altered the environment in which organizations compete. This has led to an increase in alliances or mergers between organizations with similar products or services, but dissimilar or complementary characteristics in other areas. Technological discontinuities can cause enormous difficulties for mature organizations. This is largely because radical innovation requires a large amount of resources and new knowledge. Taking advantage of complementarities in key knowledge areas through collaboration has been specifically important for innovation in sectors with high levels of complexity, such as biotechnology (Blomqvist and Levy 2006).

Rothaermel (2002) posited that alliances are increasingly preferred over mergers, acquisitions, or internal development. This is because of urgency or industry uncertainty and the need to respond to shorter product life cycles. Alliances allow organizations that lack key technologies to leverage partners' capabilities to accelerate new product development. In contrast, a merger or acquisition may face the risk of a lack of synergy emerging between the two organizations. Furthermore, an acquisition may be more costly because the acquiring organization may end up purchasing technology that is of little use. An alliance, on the other hand, allows an organization to avoid acquiring only that which is needed.

Lambe and Spekman (1997) posited that more alliances are established when urgency and uncertainty are high. Once product or market uncertainty begins to lessen, alliances may become less critical because the ongoing activity is further improved in the dominant design. At this stage, once the path of technological discontinuity ceases to be important, organizations may opt for investing in internal development. Major players may then begin to build their own vertically integrated facilities and dissolve their alliance (den Uijl and de Vries 2013).

During the mature phase of the technology life cycle, acquisitions or mergers may be more attractive than alliance because the partners may be competitors and have equal access to the technology (Briggs and Watt 2001). During the discontinuation phase, current technology may be obsoleted by new technology At this juncture, markets are often usually volatile, as innovations and next-generation products destroy the demand for prior-generation goods. New organizations may appear, and as the nature of emerging new technology becomes uncertain, the number of new alliances tends to increase. As understanding grows concerning the potential and implications associated with a new the technology, some organizations will begin to consider the creation of new alliances (Agarwal, Sarkar, and Echambadi 2002).

Playbook Guideline 67: The complexity of some technological entrepreneurship problems can only be overcome by the formation of organizational alliances

Electric Vehicles

Case Aims: To illustrate how alliances are formed to permit large incumbent firms to rapidly acquire new knowledge

Where radical innovations require new expertise, firms are likely to seek out new partners to provide this new knowledge. The resources controlled by incumbent firms make them appealing as partners. Start-ups during periods of industrial upheaval usually possess the expertise necessary to develop radical innovations. In those situations, start-ups will likely have partnership offers from firms seeking access to new expertise.

Sierzchula et al. (2015) examined car industry alliances concerned with the development of electric vehicles' manufacturers to determine which were to explorative versus exploitative alliances. In terms of firms that had experience and knowledge, seven key firms were identified, namely Coda Automotive, Leo Motors, Mia Electric, Tesla Motors, E-Wolf, Venturi, and Zap. The key knowledge areas within these firms were batteries, electric drive trains, charging and infrastructure, and new body materials. It was apparent that the large incumbent car firms formed a greater number of alliances with various of these organizations, presumably to provide themselves with an ongoing competitive advantage while concurrently exploiting their own high level of internal resources.

Purchasing Knowledge

The conventional philosophy behind M&As is one or both parties perceive the investment will provide financial benefits from the purchase price being lower than the actual company value, improving profitability through implementing postpurchase cost-cutting restructuring or exploiting economies of scale. In recent years, however, the logic behind many high-tech M&As has been to acquire new knowledge or permit access to new market sectors. Brueller, Carmeli, and Drori (2014) defined this latter approach as a "bolt-on acquisition" to support either a product or market extension into an adjacent product-market category. Other acquisitions by high-technology incumbents can be described as "technology-grafting" where the focus is on accessing capabilities in the areas of new products or technologies.

In bolt-on acquisitions, the acquirer gains important new operational process experience. This is because the main purpose of these acquisitions is to complement internal R&D efforts and allow acquirers to quickly respond to shorter product life cycles, where time-to-market is of paramount importance. One example of this strategy is provided by Facebook. In 2009, the company acquired the social media real-time news aggregator. In 2010, the Malaysian contact-importing start-up Octazen Solutions and the photo-sharing service called Divvyshot. This was followed by Facebook purchasing the photo-sharing service Instagram for approximately $1 billion and subsequently WhatsApp Inc, a smartphone instant messaging application for $19 billion (Bercovici 2014).

Carmeli and Azerual (2009) noted that, upon the implementation of an acquisition, both organizations need to develop knowledge-combination capabilities plus the ability to absorb, integrate, and exchange information. These researchers concluded that, in the context of M&As, knowledge flows enable the parties to access each other's knowledge base, but in order to promote strategic agility, they need to develop the capacity to exploit the knowledge that has been exchanged and transferred.

> *Playbook Guideline 68: In some cases, the only way to implement a technological entrepreneurial strategy is to participate in one or more M&As*

Combining Knowledge

Case Aims: To illustrate the processes associated with a merger aimed at combining knowledge capabilities

In 2001, prior to deciding that ongoing performance could best be achieved through a merger with Compaq, Hewlett Packard's (HP's) board of directors defined four potential alternative strategic development pathways for the company (Burgelman and McKinney 2006).

1. Continue along the current path: same businesses and improve performance without major acquisitions or spinouts
2. Aggressively grow services capabilities, including outsourcing and business process upgrades via acquisitions
3. Put primary focus on becoming the leading printing and imaging company

4. Become the leader in all current major business areas and become the largest IT supplier via major acquisitions

Having reviewed the options, the preferred strategy the board opted for was to initiate a merger with Compaq. This decision was followed by an analysis to generate a new corporate strategy to define how combining the two companies would improve the product-market position of the new larger entity, strengthen distinctive competences, and exploit these strengthened competences. The selected positioning for the new entity was a "high-tech, low-cost" corporate strategy. Unfortunately, for the next few years, HP encountered problems in implementing a successful strategic integration phase. Eventually, it was decided to appoint a new CEO, Mark Hurd. He focused on returning to HP's original culture of leveraging internal competences based on the organization being first and foremost being a technology-driven company (LaPlante 2007).

CHAPTER 10

The Service Sector

Sector Importance

In less than three decades after the end of World War II, manufacturing as a wealth generator has been overtaken by service sector organizations in terms of contribution to Gross Domestic Product (GDP) and as a source of employment. When service providers such as banks and insurance companies sought to achieve higher market share in the 1980s, many adopted marketing principles involving heavy reliance upon advertising and sales promotions that had proven effective for tangible goods companies such as Coca-Cola or Proctor & Gamble. Service sector promotional spending rose dramatically, but many service firms did not enjoy any real growth in market share as a result of their increased emphasis on marketing activities. This failure of branded goods marketing to be effective in the case of service sector firms led both practitioners and academics to recognize the need for new concepts and approaches in the management of service operations (Raich and Crepaz 2009).

This new focus of efforts led to recognition that services exhibit the following inherent differences relative to manufactured goods (Zeithmal and Bitner 1996):

1. *Intangibility*, which reflects the fact that many services cannot be seen, tasted, or touched in the same way that customers can sense tangible goods.

2. *Heterogeneity* due to the fact that customers often exhibit variations in the nature of their needs, and because service delivery often involves people, the quality of the service delivered by different employees may exhibit variation.

3. *Perishability* because services cannot be stored and saved for later sales; this means managing the balance between fluctuations in

supply and demand requires new approaches in the management of service delivery. Even more importantly, many services, such as empty seats on an aircraft, represent potential revenue that cannot be recovered at some later date.

4. *Simultaneous production and consumption* reflecting the fact that many services are produced and consumed with both the customer and the supplier requiring to be present in the same location.

In addition to these identified unique characteristics, an even more fundamental problem is that, in the case of many service goods, such as banking, insurance, or mass market retailing, there is often no way for a supplier to create differences in the service proposition, which permits distinguishing the offering from other suppliers in the same market sector. This situation can be contrasted with tangible goods, where attributes, such as design, appearance, or superior performance, permit suppliers to differentiate their company from competition. As a consequence, it can be argued that exploiting entrepreneurship in a service sector situation is somewhat more difficult than in a tangible goods business (Chaston 2016).

The other difficulty in differentiating the service firm from competition is the commonality in the nature of the service offering, which often means that in terms of exploiting the 4Ps of marketing (i.e., product, promotion, price, and place) in many markets, suppliers can only rely on exploiting price as a way of distinguishing their proposition from competition. Given the limitations of exploiting the 4Ps in service sector firms to build market share, additional variables have been recognized as a route through which to assist differentiation of benefit propositions in the market place. The three commonest additional variables that may provide an opportunity for entrepreneurial enhancement of the traditional marketing mix are as follows (Magrath 1986):

1. *People* who are all of the individuals associated with any aspect of supplying, delivering, or interacting with the customer during the service provision process
2. *Processes,* which are the procedures, mechanisms, activities, and systems associated with the creation and delivery of a service

3. *Physical evidence,* which is constituted of all the physical elements of the environment in which customer interaction and service provision occurs

Playbook Guideline 69: The unique characteristics of service markets means exploiting technological entrepreneurship to differentiate the organization from competition can be extremely difficult

Breaking Market Convention

Case Aims: To illustrate how in a long-established service sector a new distribution system can be radically altered by an entrepreneurial proposition

In 1994, Jeff Bezos identified the Internet as an entrepreneurial opportunity through which to create a new approach to retailing that did not involve terrestrial outlets. Bezos determined that the five most-promising products for online distribution were compact disks, computer hardware, computer software, videos, and books. He selected books as the first online product proposition based on large worldwide mass market demand for literature, books' low prices, and the huge number of titles available. The major advantage of selling books online was that, while the largest brick and mortar bookstores and mail order catalogs might offer up to 200,000 titles, his online bookstore Amazon.com could offer an even wider selection because of the ability to operate out of a virtual warehouse while relying upon publishers to store actual products (Harris 2011).

Through his actions, Bezos demonstrated to the world the huge entrepreneurial opportunities available from taking service sector propositions online.

It is probable that the most successful service sector innovations are those that concurrently reduce operating costs through achieving a high scale of operations while sustaining customer value. Bezos clearly understood this fact as demonstrated by his strategy of moving overseas, expanding the product line beyond books and permitting affiliates to market their products via the Amazon website, and more recently, offering cloud computing and Big Data management services.

Customer Satisfaction

Ultimately, the success of organizations is dependent on delivering customer satisfaction. Usually, this can only occur when the customer's expectations are equaled or even exceeded by their actual perceptions generated during the purchase and consumption process. The advantage in the case of tangible goods is the existence of defined product specifications that guide the manufacturing process, and the quality control systems permit rectification of product quality problems before goods are shipped. This will usually ensure customer expectations are matched by perceptions. Variables such as intangibility, the heterogeneous needs of customers, and the potential variation in behavior among employees engaged in service provision means achievement of the same outcome is much more difficult. As a consequence, service quality is a critically important issue in service markets and can, in some cases, provide the basis for differentiating the supplier from competition (Mayer, Erhart, and Schneider 2009).

The key objective in delivering service quality satisfaction is to minimize the gap between customers' desires and actual experience (i.e., the gap between what they hope will happen and what actually occurs). Research by Parasuraman, Zeithaml, and Berry (1988) led to the development of a model named SERVQUAL for assessing the effectiveness and quality of the service provision process. Their research identified the following variables, which could be used to categorize customer expectations:

1. *Reliability,* which is the ability to perform the promised service dependably and accurately
2. *Tangibles,* which are the images created by the appearance of physical facilities, equipment, personnel, and communication materials
3. *Responsiveness,* which is the willingness to help customers and provide prompt service
4. *Assurance,* which is by the process by which the knowledge, ability, and courtesy of employees engenders customer trust and confidence in the service provider
5. *Empathy,* which is created by the caring, individualized attention, which employees offer the customer

The conventional use of SERVQUAL data is to identify ways of minimizing the gap between customer perceptions and expectations. The entrepreneurial service firm can be expected to pursue a more farsighted objective of (a) removing the gap completely and (b) where feasible, implementing actions to ensure the actual service experience totally exceeds customer expectations. In the case of a pure play online service provider, the basic SERVQUAL model will provide the information to determine whether actions need to be implemented to enhance the service quality. The potential problem facing a "clicks and mortar provider" is that factors influencing customer expectations may differ between online and terrestrial situations. In those cases where this is thought to apply, the organization will need to modify the SERVQUAL model to accommodate the need to differentiate between different types of customers. One such approach is illustrated in Figure 10.1 in which the organization will need to assume that the following gaps exist:

Gap 1a not comprehending the actual expectations of terrestrial customers.

Gap 1b not comprehending the actual expectations of online customers.

Gap 2a a failure to translate perceptions of terrestrial customer expectations into service quality standards.

Gap 2b a failure to translate perceptions of online customer expectations into service quality standards.

Gap 3a a lack of resources or inadequately skilled employees results in an inability to deliver services which meet terrestrial performance standards.

Gap 3b a lack of resources or inadequately skilled employees results in an inability to deliver services which meet online performance standards.

Gap 4a communicating information to customers via terrestrial channels which causes them to be misled or misunderstand service provision.

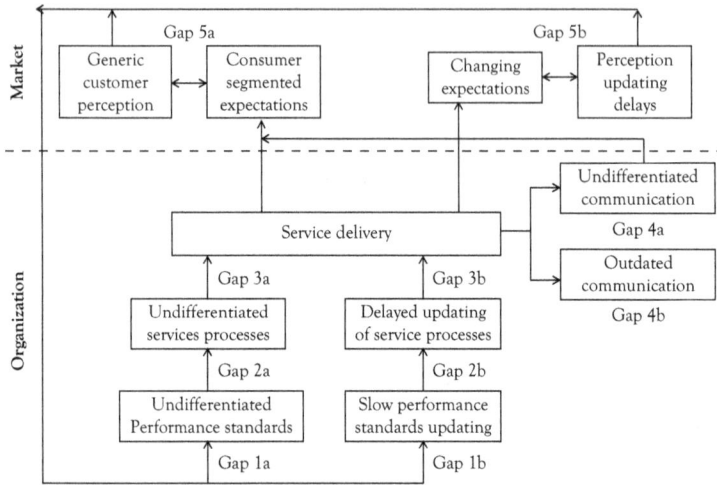

Figure 10.1 Gap-based quality factors in financial services provision

Gap 4b communicating information to customers via social media channels which causes them to be misled or misunderstand service provision.

Gap 5a a combination of Gaps 1a to 4a determining terrestrial customers overall assessment of how their expectations have been met.

Gap 5b a combination of Gaps 1b to 4b determining online customers overall assessment of how their expectations have been met.

In terms of online services, the provider has many more opportunities to exploit a strategy of delivering superior service quality. This is because the organization is in a more informed position by exploiting real-time data to assess customer expectations versus perceptions and evaluate all aspects of the service delivery process by analyzing website analytics, product returns, and customer complaints. In those cases where performance is inadequate, the organization has various options such as website automation, revising back office systems, investing in training, adding more staff, or seeking to further automate certain aspects of the service delivery process. Further enhancement of customer understanding can be achieved by undertaking market research accompanied by regular assessments of employee attitudes and motivation (Chaston 2015).

Piccoli, Brohman, and Parasuraman (2004) proposed that online firms will exploit technology to create more innovative services and enhance the effectiveness of customer interaction. As technology is increasingly used to provide a widening array of innovative support services, customers may develop a perception of the higher level of service quality being delivered. A key reason for this outcome is automated support services that provide a means of supplying the missing "human touch" by leveraging IT to provide multiple assistance, which, in many cases, could not realistically be delivered in an offline setting.

Playbook Guideline 70: A key source for exploiting technological entrepreneurship is to leverage IT to achieve or deliver a superior service experience

Meeting Customer Expectations

Case Aims: To illustrate how entrepreneurial solutions can ensure avoidance of service gaps and thereby ensure customer expectations are fulfilled

Once a firm comprehends the nature of customer expectations, then one way of ensuring that these expectations are always exceeded is to set operating standards well above those used by conventional competitors. Starbucks, which is a chain of coffee houses now operating in a number of countries around the world, started life in 1971 as a single gourmet coffee store in Seattle, Washington. The cornerstone upon which the company's success was founded is an obsession with brewing the best possible cup of coffee. To embed these standards into all employees, the company runs extensive training programs during which participants are briefed in detail on every aspect of the Starbuck operation. Additionally, during these sessions, employees are educated about the world of coffee in order to permit them hold informed conversations with their customers. To further enhance customer dialog by building on the firm's role as a social gathering place, the company has become an entrepreneurial leader in the exploitation of the social media. These activities involve services maintained by the firm (e.g., MyStarbucks Idea) and via third-party services such as Facebook, Twitter, YouTube, and Foursquare.

Further customer interaction has been achieved through the exploitation of mobile devices. Starbucks has collaborated with Apple, distributing weekly iTunes songs, offering a custom Starbucks iTunes channel, and integrating in-store music to display a Starbucks button in iTunes for further sampling and purchase. An iPhone app provides store menus, nutrition information, store locators, card management, and even payment facilities. While the success of these efforts varies, they collectively underscore the firm's willingness to experiment (Gallaugher 2010).

Competitive Advantage

Hamel and Pralahad (1994) proposed that the relevance of resource-based view (RBV) theory in high-tech service industries is validated by an organization's ability to assemble a bundle of skills and technologies that permit the organization to develop a unique, new technology platform. These authors suggest an example of this perspective is provided by the case of Microsoft. The company's core competence in the development of new software platforms has permitted the company to become the dominant provider of software installed in both business and home PCs. Furthermore, having achieved market dominance for a specific business platform, Microsoft has greatly increased the probability that newly acquired internal competences will provide the basis for further market growth and the launch of new products.

Kay (1993) noted that the problems associated with establishing a viable differentiation strategy in service markets means the RBV theory has significant appeal in terms of focusing management attention on internal capabilities as the basis for achieving competitive advantage. One way of applying the RBV theory in service firms is to examine which of the additional "3Ps" of people, process, or physical evidence could provide the basis for offering a proposition seen as more appealing than competitors' offerings. Kay suggested strategy is about relating the organization's core competences to external environments, and that to be successful, competitive advantage must be sustainable, and where feasible, also be unique. He suggested there are four potential sources of strength available to an organization, namely reputation, innovation, internal and external relationships, and organizational assets.

In the case of service organizations where benefit differentiation is difficult to achieve, a usual strategic philosophy is to focus either on offering superior quality or a lower-cost proposition. This strategic positioning dimension can often be enhanced by deciding whether to have the capacity to deliver transactional services to a large number of customers or alternatively to focus on making highly accurate, specialist customized services available to a selective group of customers (Goyal and Srivastava 2015).

Playbook Guideline 71: Where benefit differentiation is difficult, technological entrepreneurs may need to focus on developing one or more new superior organizational competences

Financial Services

Long before the advent of the Internet, the financial services industry had been using electronic data interchange systems to manage the flow of information between institutions and clients. The industry was one of the first to identify the opportunities offered by the storage, access, and transfer of data using computers. The Internet was soon recognized as providing new opportunities to lower costs by exploiting this medium in place of channels such as the telephone, fax, or cable-linked computer networks. As broadband speeds have improved, this has assisted organizations, such as banks, to migrate their customers from terrestrial to online transactions, and thereby, reduce operating costs (Allen, McAndres, and Strahan 2002).

Some banks have used technology for redesigning business processes, providing new products and services, and improving the organizational work environment. Guimaraes, Bransford, and Guimaraes (2010) concluded that in the banking sector, successful innovation requires knowledge of the best technology available, effective use of specific technologies, and benchmarking the use of specific technologies relative to competition.

Playbook Guideline 72: Technological entrepreneurship provides new pathways through which financial services firms can deliver enhanced service or reduce transaction costs

Business Model Innovation

Most service sector firms operate within long-established supply chains to deliver customer satisfaction. Gaining access to these supply chains can be difficult for a new entrant, and the possibility of entrenched conservative values among supply chain members or the final customer may prove a barrier to successfully launching a highly innovative new service. Hence, it may be necessary to consider switching to a different supply chain, or alternatively, creating an entirely new supply chain. The advent of the Internet, as illustrated by Amazon.com's impact on terrestrial retailing, has been one of the most important technological changes that has provided new business model opportunities for innovation across many service industry sectors.

Koen, Bertels, and Elsum (2011) proposed that business model information typology (BMIT) permits classification of innovation along the three dimensions of technology, value network, and resolution of any financial hurdles. They further divided the innovation space into two zones, sustaining innovation and business model innovation. Within the technology dimension, they identified three types of technologies, namely incremental, architectural, and radical technological innovation. Architectural innovation is about creating new ways to integrate components in a system to permit incremental changes to an existing technology. An example of architectural innovation is the iPod, which was not based on entirely new technology, but did represent an entirely new design.

The value network dimension encompasses how a firm identifies, works with, and reacts to members of the supply chain. Relationships can be a critical source of competitive advantage. Business model innovation often requires the development of a new value network involving a different supply chain and the creation of new relationships within this supply chain.

Playbook Guideline 73: Service sector technological entrepreneurship may require the creation of a new business model in order to be successful

Remodeling the Music Industry

Case Aims: To illustrate how new technology has provided new entrepreneurial opportunities in the music industry

For many years, the music industry was dominated by a small number of record companies that controlled the market and determined which recording artists would receive promotional support. The advent of Internet, MP3, and peer-to-peer (P2P) networks dramatically altered this business model, with recorded music evolving from a physical entity to a digital good accessed online through search and sampling software. Today's albums can actually be playlists self-created by consumers based on their own tastes and preferences. New services, such as Apple, Yahoo, eMusic, have emerged to offer digital songs (Bhattacharjee et al. 2009).

As online music has become the dominant product form, artists and musicians have recognized the power of new technologies, that is, it may be feasible to survive without depending upon a record company supporting and promoting them. Increasingly new and well-established artists are making their products available online themselves, and hence, are no longer dependent on a contract with a major label as the only pathway through which to achieve commercial success. The music industry has recognized the profit potential for product extensions or peripherals, such as ringtones and call back tones, music within video games, music within social networking sites, and personalized playlists. However, the music industry has not been able to corner this market because they face competition from a multitude of market intermediaries, wireless carriers, game developers, and online service entities.

The change in the industry is an excellent example of Christensen's (1997) view of disruptive innovation whereby industry disruption through new players has dramatically reduced prices. Downloading thrives on the Internet not only because it can be free, but also because it offers unlimited scope and endless selection. It was not until 2008 that the major recording firms agreed to open up their catalogs of rights. This action supported the development of new subscription models based on the concept of "bundling" music with other services or devices using an Internet Service Provider (ISP) subscription, a mobile phone, or a portable player. While the music comes virtually "free" to consumers under this model (e.g., www.spotify.com), record companies and artists get paid a percentage from the sale of services or devices.

Productivity

Ultimately, the performance of any organization is determined by the productivity of the employees relative to other organizations engaged in the provision of the same goods and services (Rust and Huang 2012). Employees are often the highest cost component in many organizations. Hence, it is not surprising that entrepreneurs and organizations have sought ways whereby the employee can be replaced by automation. However, automation is rarely a low-cost option because organizations are required to make significant investments in new capital equipment. Compared to the tangible goods sector, service organizations have achieved much less success in exploiting mechanization and automation to improve productivity. In part, this reflects the need to employ people to provide the interface between the supplier and the market when servicing heterogeneous customer needs. Another factor is that, in certain service sectors, such as the fast-food industry, low skills' individuals can be recruited and paid a minimum wage.

Playbook Guideline 74: Technological entrepreneurship may provide an opportunity to exploit automation to reduce service sector operating costs

The IT Revolution

The arrival of the Internet offered the potential of instant access to information, and the ability to order products and services online on a 24/7 basis totally changed the nature and future opportunities in virtually every service industry sector. More recently, the advent of mobile technology, such as the smartphone, has further altered, and in some cases, completely changed the dynamics and nature of supplier–customer inter-action within service markets. Wright and Dawood (2009) noted it was not until the 21st century that the necessary advances were in place across computing, electronic communications, and exploitation of the Internet to permit effective exploitation of IT within many service sectors. This new era, which has been labeled by some as the "smart age" (Anon 2010), offers new opportunities to those service firms that have the core compe-tences in the area of acquiring and analyzing very large datasets, thereby permitting exploitation of smart-age technology for creating a competitive advantage based on a superior understanding of customer needs.

In order to exploit advances in technology to evolve new paradigms for delivering services, enhancing customer satisfaction, or improving productivity, service firms must comprehend the nature of the latest advances in digital technologies and how these can provide the basis for implementing fundamental organizational change. The problem facing many service operations, especially those in more mature industries, such as retailing or banking, is that the senior management may lack sufficient technological knowledge to determine whether the latest advances can deliver the cost and benefit outcomes that are being claimed. It is for these reasons the entry point should be that of seeking to determine how new technology may impact a future service strategy based around assessing the role of people in the delivery of processes.

Playbook Guideline 75: The advent of the smart age has opened up a whole new range of ways through which technological entrepreneurship can be exploited by service firms

CHAPTER 11

Health Care

Introduction

In terms of the world's metaproblems, one of the greatest is the continuing rising costs of health care provision. The factors influencing this cost spiral include (i) ongoing advances in medical technology, (ii) rising levels of obesity, and (iii) population aging. This latter factor is critical because older people face expensive illnesses, such as cancer; heart conditions; and mental problems, such as dementia. In those cases where a government funds a major proportion of health care provision, the financial burden is approaching the point where ongoing affordability has become an unmanageable burden for the welfare state. Similarly, where health care is funded through medical insurance, premiums have become a massive burden for employers or individuals. As a consequence, governments and employers recognize that change must occur, which results in making health care provision more cost-effective and patient-orientated. The potentially most effective strategy for affecting a change probably lies within greater exploitation of entrepreneurship. McCleary et al. (2006) opined, on the basis of current and emerging trends in health care, that entrepreneurial opportunities exist across the continuum of care.

Playbook Guideline 76: Technological entrepreneurship can make a critical contribution to halting rising costs within the health care sector

Specialist Knowledge

In the health care sector, new solutions often require an in-depth knowledge of the situation confronting the medical professional. As a consequence, equipment manufacturers are often not in a position to initiate radical innovation, but instead become involved in commercialization after a medical professional has validated the technological viability of a new proposition. To gain further understanding of radical innovation in the health care sector, Lett et al. (2006) undertook a study to generate knowledge in relation to the four different projects. In all four cases, initial users were the originators of the radical innovation. Their common problem was the most effective procedures could not be undertaken using standard neurosurgical instruments. This is reflective of the fact that major medical problems are a key source for creative activities (Collins and Amabile 1999). In addition to problem-induced motivation, all surgeons were professionals in their field, and thus, had in-depth knowledge within their domain of surgery. Furthermore, they had knowledge about the respective needs to improve the surgical process. This knowledge was gained by extensive learning, experience, and experimentation, which is difficult and costly to transfer to third parties (Von Hippel 1998). During the idea-creation and concept-generation processes of the innovation, surgeons followed a common pattern of searching for appropriate technologies outside of the medical domain. They applied analogical reasoning in involvement in searching out new ideas and concepts. This situation caused Lett et al. to propose that it is often the case that, in the health care sector, it is users rather than manufacturing firms who are more likely to develop radically new concepts.

Playbook Guideline 77: In the health care sector, it is often those with specialist medical knowledge who are the originators of technological entrepreneurial solutions

Biotechnology

Although surgery has remained an important aspect of medical treatments, other key advances such as the development of inoculations and vaccines to provide resistance to diseases, drugs such as sulfonamides, and antibiotics such as penicillin have provided new forms of medical care. Since the 1920s, drug-based solutions have provided the basis for the evolution of a global pharmaceutical industry. The problem is the high price of drugs, and the monopoly position allowed through the granting of patents, means this area of treatment has become one of the largest costs facing the health care industry (Müller, Fujiwara, and Herstatt 2004).

Pharmaceutical firms face strong pressures to develop medicines for a global market and exploit economies of scale. Fleming and Sorenson (2004) noted that the growing interdependence of previously discrete technologies creates difficulties for any single firm wishing to stand alone in the industry Thus, R&D alliances play a critical role in this industry, in which alliance-based teams race toward the creation and commercialization of similar end-products and a winner-takes-all situation may often exist.

Biotechnology has enabled pharmaceutical firms to move from a random approach to conducting a rational design approach, in which compounds are developed from scientific theories regarding the origins and evolution of diseases. The latter approach means that pharmaceutical firms must rely on science more than ever before (Cockburn, Henderson, and Stern 2000).

This new technology represents an important area of medical innovation as an alternative to reliance upon drugs developed by the major pharmaceutical firms. The science involves the use of living systems and organisms to develop or make products. Application fields of biotechnology are as diverse as health care, chemistry, material science, agriculture, and environmental protection. In the United States alone, there now exists a huge number of biotech companies, most of which are extremely small and are perceived as an important path through which to challenge the semimonopoly position of the major pharmaceutical companies.

In recent years, advances in biotechnology have led to new and diverse sciences such as genomics, recombinant gene techniques, applied immunology, and development of pharmaceutical therapies and diagnostic tests. The technology is based on biological or biotechnology concepts to harness cellular and biomolecular processes to develop technologies and products that deliver new forms of medical treatment. Over the past three decades, biotechnology has emerged as a vital global industry associated with a sustained flow of innovations dramatically improving human health (Gans and Stern 2004).

Until the early 1980s, the prevailing belief was that no new company could compete with the pharmaceutical industry giants because of the enormous costs of developing the necessary R&D infrastructure. However, biotech firms have not only challenged the traditional pharmaceutical companies as the discoverers and developers of new products, but also have built credibility in novel areas such as cell biology, molecular genetics, and drug delivery. Biotechnology companies operate amid uncertainty and rapid change. Fuchs and Krauss (2003) posited that biotech firms are unique. First, they are strongly science-based, more nimble, and less risk-averse than pharmaceutical companies with innovation within these firms often far more radical. Second, biotech companies represent a source of tacit knowledge with the exploitation of knowledge requiring intense science-based interactions. Alliances with other biotech firms, university research centers, and pharmaceutical companies are the norm in the industry, providing biotech with faster access to capital and knowledge, enabling companies to react more quickly and flexibly to new developments and offering better protection for intellectual property rights. However, the timeline between establishing the company and product launch is usually very long. On average, the entire biotech process, from scientific discovery to commercialization, can take up to 15 years. This reality exposes entrepreneurs to a plethora of critical and time-sensitive decisions. As a consequence, failure rates among biotech firms are relatively high.

Playbook Guideline 78: Biotechnology offers a huge new field of opportunity for exploiting technological entrepreneurship in the treatment of medical conditions

Genomics

In genetics and genomics, the sequencing of the human genome has resulted in the development of new biological drugs to treat cancer and other serious diseases. So-called "targeted therapeutics" is the first step in creating drugs that attack a disease without affecting healthy cells and tissues. Leading firms and research institutes are switching their focus from genetics to genomics. A genomics program focuses attention away from individual mutations, individual genes, and individual patients to next-generation sequencing of genomes and storing genomic profiles of thousands of mutations across tens of thousands of patients in a biobank. These data provide knowledge to undertake research spanning the disease spectrum (Reinke 2015). The perceived potential of genomics was a catalyst for numerous new entrepreneurial start-ups in the 1990s. Many of these firms struggled to survive, and hence, this has necessitated the development of new business models to generate adequate revenue flows to support ongoing research.

Genome sequencing is very efficient and increasingly cost-effective, permitting innovations in disease prediction, detection, and treatment. As a consequence, genomics companies have sought to leverage their position by "adding value" to their proprietary assets. For example, a database can be annotated, a microchip can be engineered to measure a wider range of parameters more sensitively or with greater accuracy, and some types of assets can be customized to meet the needs of particular clients or partners within a research alliance. Rothman and Kraft (2006) noted that to increase revenue streams, young, genomics start-ups have turned to utilizing alliances to achieve long-term survival.

While target identification provided a vital initial market for genomics companies, this had short-lived commercial viability. Rothman and Kraft concluded there were two main reasons for this outcome. First, the increased availability of DNA sequencing technologies and sequence databases had, by the late 1990s, reduced their use to that of a "commodity technology." Second, target generation and screening technologies, especially combinatorial chemistry (CC) and high-throughput screening (HTS) systems, have been developed to automate and accelerate the speed with which the genome could be searched and targets identified. These advances were immediately adopted by the big existing pharmaceutical companies either through investment in the technology or by company acquisition.

In their review of the declining revenue, Rothman and Kraft noted that genomics companies have developed a number of means through which they are able to differentiate their products, add value to the supply chain, and thus, leverage their position in commercial negotiations. One solution has been move downstream. This has been achieved by establishing internal drug development programs (IDDPs), permitting these firms to leverage their biological expertise and discovery capabilities. Some of these companies also have established IDDPs by using in-licensed compounds from pharmaceutical or biotechnology companies. Others have combined in-licensing with the use of internally generated compounds to achieve greater control within a drug development program. These changes are necessary to cope with the problem that the regulatory and structural framework of the drug innovation cycle is often very lengthy. However, where these firms have such a have drug candidate that has passed through preclinical trials, then this commands a much higher commercial value. In moving downstream, the genomics companies are adding shareholder value because they now own drugs that are nearer to being marketed to the health care sector.

Playbook Guideline 79: Genomics offers huge new opportunities for exploiting technological entrepreneurship in the treatment of medical conditions

Digital Technology

The Internet and related communications technologies are seen as the most likely source of entrepreneurial solutions, whereby a reduction in the costs of health care services might be achieved. This is because the Internet can provide the following benefits (Riva 2000):

1. Establishing close, supportive relationships with patients
2. Becoming the preferred source of health information and service provision
3. Increasing patient convenience
4. Creating more effective ways to share knowledge and information
5. Creating new ways to deliver care
6. Reducing operating expenses by applying IT-based automation

The Internet and related communications technology have massive potential for supporting the provision of health care through activities such as transmitting data from a remote location for response by a health care professional based at a central location and by health care professionals offering treatment guidance to medical staff located elsewhere within a country. However, developing countries often depend heavily on private profit-orientated entities for provision of health care services. This situation has attracted some medical entrepreneurs driven by a desire to serve disadvantaged sections of the society by attempting to provide accessible and affordable services to the masses by innovatively designing economically sustainable business models. In both developed and developing nations, IT is one of the prime resources leveraged to enhance service delivery. Srivastava and Shainesh (2015) posited that, in addition to ICT, which is the key interactional resource in most health care value-creation systems, there is a need to continually search for and orchestrate contextually available knowledge and institutional resources to deliver the desired value.

Playbook Guideline 80: Digital technology offers numerous ways through which to exploit entrepreneurship as a pathway for reducing health care delivery costs

Delivering Cost-Effective Health Care

Case Aims: To illustrate how the entrepreneurial exploitation of technology can support cost-effectiveness in health care provision

Srivastava and Shainesh (2015) examined the activities of AECS Ltd in India to gain an understanding of value provision by exploiting IT in developing country health care provision. Dr. Venkataswamy founded AECS in Madurai as a private nonprofit eye hospital that would provide eye care at an affordable price. His mission was to eradicate unnecessary blindness, and Dr. Venkataswamy pioneered a high-volume, cost-effective, high-quality eye care system by adopting a delivery model based on the standardization principle that trains people anywhere in the world to efficiently produce the same product. AECS has grown to become one of the largest eye care delivery systems in the world and has conducted almost four million surgeries over a span of three and a half decades.

   In 2012, AECS's nine hospitals treated about 2.8 million outpatients and conducted more than 300,000 surgeries. Dr. Venkataswamy believed that high volume was the key to achieving low cost and making eye care affordable, thereby delivering eye care to millions of Indians.

This achievement entails reaching out to patients in rural areas, rather than waiting for them to visit urban hospitals. AECS organizes weekend "eye camps" involving the establishment of temporary eye clinics in rural areas for routine eye checkups and simple medical procedures. Patients requiring further specialized treatment or surgery are taken to AECS's base hospitals, and three to four days after treatment, are transported back home. The surgeons at AECS each perform more than 2,000 surgeries every year, compared with the national average of 400 surgeries per surgeon.

AECS's telemedicine initiative is aimed at efficiently reaching the rural masses and providing quality service at affordable prices. The trained technicians at the VC diagnosis centers identify common eye problems, dispense spectacles, and treat minor injuries after consulting with the base hospital ophthalmologist using low-cost broadband. The technician has the patient sit in front of a digital camera, thus enabling the patient to speak to the specialist at the base hospital who provides real-time consultations. The center's coordinator manages patient registration with electronic medical records (EMR) on the networked computer, provides optical services, maintains accounts, manages the inventory of supplies, provides counseling, and coordinates referrals with the base hospital. The EMR is a permanent history of the patient, which enables the technician and the ophthalmologist at the base hospital to access medical records efficiently. This real-time teleconnectivity decouples eye care service into three interconnected, but distinct components, namely (1) the patient examination by the VC technician, (2) diagnosis by the specialist at the base hospital, and (3) dispensation of medicine and/or spectacles by the VC technician. This decoupling facilitates effective utilization of the specialists' time and skills, resulting in much greater overall systemic efficiency.

Helpful Technology*

Case Aims: To illustrate how entrepreneurial exploitation of the Internet is enhancing the effectiveness and efficiency of health care provision

UPMC

At University Pittsburgh Medical Center (UPMC) in Pittsburgh, an innovative tool, eVisit app, is facilitating online interactions between patients and physicians that can eliminate the need for a visit to a physician's office, urgent care center, or emergency department. The app allows patients of UPMC physicians who have signed onto the health system's patient portal to complete a detailed questionnaire from any Internet-enabled device regarding their ailments. Patients receive a response quickly often within minutes, and usually within about four hours. If a prescription is required, the order is transmitted electronically to the patient's pharmacy. The price for an eVisit is $40. Approximately, 400 primary care and internal medicine physicians participate in the eVisits system.

Baptist Health

Two years ago, Baptist Health South Florida designed "FineApp" to help patients quickly scan the "door-to-doctor" wait times at nearby emergency departments (EDs) and urgent care center in the Baptist Health network and to access driving directions and contact information for the facilities from a mobile phone or iPad. Wait times are provided in 15-minute intervals for urgent care centers and one-hour intervals for hospital EDs. The system device makes it easy for people who are in need of urgent or emergency care to see what the wait times are in deciding where to go for treatment.

Janes Philip Medical Center

At 135-bed Jane Philips Medical Center in Bartlesville, Oklahoma, nurses are avoiding medication errors and adverse drug events with the help of an app they can access from an iPod or Touchpad. Nurses carry the devices in their pockets. When medications are administered, they use the device to scan the barcode of each drug, then scan the patient's barcode and wait for the device to signal that the right medication is being given to the right patient at the right time, using information from the patient's electronic health record for verification. The app also has the capability to track specimen collection, infant care regimens, care interventions, and care team communications and to view and manage the patient's care plan.

* *Source:* Williams 2012.

Medical Data

A major component of the health care provision is the acquisition, storage, and analysis of data. At the level of the individual patient, this activity occurs when a medical professional engages in a review of symptoms, examines past medical history, or assesses the prognosis of ongoing treatment. Exploitation of available data also occurs at the macrolevel, such as a hospital, utilizing patient records to evaluate alternative treatment regimes or at a national or international level when determining the effectiveness of an illness prevention program, such as vaccinating children. Entrepreneurial utilization of the Internet, by providing new forms of communication and information, can offer major cost savings in relation to the management of patient data because health care professionals can access dispersed databases and exchange data on medical treatments undertaken at different locations (Binshan and Umon 2002).

Lanterman (2015) predicted the ongoing revolution in information technology in health care will to lead to advances in detection, monitoring, and treatment of a multitude of health conditions. New modes of data collection and access are changing the way that health care professionals and their patients communicate with one another. New patient-side consumer devices are revising the method and frequency of what kinds of data can be collected and transmitted. Many health care devices, both in-clinic and patient-side, can be described as belonging to the "Internet of Things."

Within the health care sector, there has been a huge push toward interoperability and interconnectedness. The latest health-related devices are being supplied with full Internet connectivity, allowing them to be remotely administered via wireless data transmission. Consumers are also keen to purchase an ever-increasing array of apps and devices that allow them to track their health habits and vitals. These new devices, including blood pressure monitors, scales, breathalyzers, toothbrushes, and their associated apps, can now track an individual's daily habits and patterns (Boos et al. 2013).

Lanterman noted that the appeal for wearable devices is demonstrated by the growing market demand for products such Apple Watch (www. apple.com), FitBit (www.fitbit.com), and Microsoft Band (www.micro-soft.com/microsoft-band). These new devices allow individuals to not only track their own habits, conditions, and exercise, but also share this information with third parties. For example, the Apple Watch's Research-Kit (www.apple.com/researchkit/technology) allows third-party app developers to tap into Apple's hardware sensors, specifically those that track a user's medical condition.

Medical researchers have developed apps to study patients with asthma, diabetes, and Parkinson's disease, thereby giving these researchers and physicians in these areas more data than was previously available. In relation to primary care, doctors are no longer reliant upon an occasional visit to the patient's home or by the patient coming to their practice. Health care providers can now have access to a person's medical condition more frequently and over extended periods of time. Another technological advance is telemedicine, which allows patients from the comfort of their own homes to telecommute to their doctor's office (Gilman and Stensland 2103).

In the past, health care providers and governments have been very enamored by the claims of the huge savings that could be made by creating national electronic records systems. Unfortunately, to-date, most of the attempts to build such systems have led to massive cost overruns and created systems not fit for purpose. This has led to a shift toward the development of electronic personal health record (PHR) systems. This alternative approach is designed to permit individuals to access, manage, and share their health information in a confidential environment (Steele et al. 2012).

The number of health care providers, who consider PHRs as a main source of information in the delivery of care, remains relatively low. This possibly reflects unfortunate experiences when using pre-Internet systems where there were problems over data reliability and adverse cost and benefit outcomes. The latter obstacle can be expected to be removed as individuals and organizations move toward storing information in the cloud. Another catalyst for change is the move toward smartcard-based PHRs and ability to access records using mobile devices.

Playbook Guideline 81: Digitization of patient records offers numerous pathways for exploiting entrepreneurship to enhance the effectiveness and efficiency of patient care

CHAPTER 12

Emerging Futures

Introduction

Attempting to accurately predict which advances in science or technology will become the foundation upon which a new source of industrial wealth generation will be built is virtually impossible. Hence, all that any futurist can hope to achieve is to identify which fields of endeavor have the potential to provide the basis for disrupting existing organizations or creating a new to the world proposition, which will eventually evolve into a total new sector of industry. Nevertheless, what is feasible is to identify areas of science and technology that may offer the potential to support upgrading existing sectors or create entirely new sector as a result of the activities of technological entrepreneurs. Hence, the purpose of this final chapter is to review some of the opportunities and global problems requiring resolution, which may become the basis of significant wealth generation at some time in the 21st century (Barrett et al. 2015).

Global Warming

It could be reasonably argued that the greatest threat facing the human race in the 21st century is global warming. A reduction in the rate of global warming demands a reduction in the level of greenhouse gas emissions. Key opportunities in this area include the expanded use of renewable energy and an improvement in the processes for the storage and distribution of electricity generated by renewables. Progress in relation to the later issue is somewhat slower than in technological advances in relation to renewable energy. This is due to the fact that, in many countries, electrical grids are often fragmented and poorly suited to achieving distribution of renewable-generated electricity (Cohen 2015). Problems include traditional electrical systems being centralized with electricity being generated at a large-scale power plant and transmitted to customers. The alternative technological opportunity is to move to distributed generation from renewable sources at or near the point of consumption combined with advances in load management and energy storage systems. Such actions would reduce the amount of energy lost in transmitting electricity and reduce the size and number of power lines needed.

PricewaterhouseCoopers (2008) described cleantech as "*not one tidy group, but rather an array of distinct sub-sectors: solar, wind, and geothermal energy generation, biofuels, energy storage (power supplies such as batteries and uninterruptible power supplies), nuclear, new pollution-abatement, recycling, clean coal, and water technologies.*" The common thread across many cleantech applications is these subsectors represent technologies, services, or products aimed at reducing greenhouse gas emissions and other pollutants and promoting energy efficiency and the conservation of natural resources. Firms in the cleantech industry are dedicated to finding technological solutions to energy, ecological, and industrial processes while growing economies and improving environmental productivity. Energy-related companies make up the largest cleantech segment, with energy being broken down into supply-side and demand-side technologies. Energy generation is probably the most well known as a result of the emergence of new technologies in relation to products such as wind turbines, batteries, electric cars, and solar panels. Other areas within the cleantech taxonomy include commercial lighting, programmable thermostats, intelligent network devices, materials, recycling, water and air purification.

For existing organizations, legislation and individual commitment to reducing greenhouse gas emission opportunities do exist to exploit innovation. The primary focus is on revising or modernizing the production processes. In energy-intensive industries such as chemicals, mining, metals, utilities, and oil and gas, new energy-efficient technologies are being developed and implemented to achieve emission reductions (Kolk and Pinkse 2005). Companies have the option of drawing upon organizational capabilities as well by exploring new product or market combinations. One possible way to enter new markets is by becoming involved in a strategic alliance with other companies, such as that now occurring in oil and automobile companies in relation to the development of fuel cells.

Another solution is to ensure that activities and sources of high emissions are carried out elsewhere in the supply chain.

Playbook Guideline 82: Technological entrepreneurship offers numerous opportunities for existing and new organizations to develop solutions for combating climate changes

Agriculture

Global warming is having a dramatic adverse impact on food production in areas such as East Africa. As a consequence, increasing emphasis is being given to the exploitation of new technology to enhance agricultural productivity. These activities involve moving beyond simple rain-fed farming techniques and harnessing water resources for food production through investment in technologies to store water, measure, and control flows for irrigation. One approach is known as "smart water management," which focuses on exploiting new technologies to enhance the effectiveness and efficiency of crop irrigation systems (Kay 2011).

Much of the pioneering in smart water management is being undertaken in developed nations such as the United States and Israel. This technology is often quite expensive, and hence, at the moment, usage will tend to be restricted to farms generating a high value from crop production. As much as 50 percent of the water applied to crops by farmers may be lost by evaporation, wind drift, and run-off, or because too much water is applied and the water sinks below the level required by plants' roots. To overcome these problems, U.S. irrigation equipment manufacturers, such as Lindsay Corporation, have developed smart irrigation systems, such as overhead water sprinklers, to reduce water loss (O'Driscoll 2012).

For hundreds of years, one way of improving crop yields has been to modify the genetic makeup of plants using techniques such as selective breeding and hybridization. This has led to the creation of "super-hybrids," which has permitted the seed companies to offer farmers the opportunity to achieve greater productivity. More recently, advances in biotechnology have resulted in the creation of genetically modified (GM) crops using a laboratory process whereby the DNA of one species are extracted and artificially introduced into the genes of an unrelated plant. The foreign

DNA may come from bacteria, viruses, insects, animals, or even humans (Qaim 2005).

The range of desirable crop traits that could potentially be developed using biotechnology is very wide, ranging from biotic and abiotic stress resistances, higher yields, better nutrient efficiency, and the ability to farm new plants. As a consequence, GM crops have been seen as beneficial not just in developed nations, but even more importantly, as a vital way of upgrading food production in poorer nations across the world. So far, however, only very few GM crop strains have been commercialized. A key obstacle is biotechnology research plus the testing and approval procedures are expensive. This means large commercial markets are required to recover the initial investment. These tend to be restricted to major crops grown on farms in developed nations. The other obstacle to expansion of usage has been that concerns among the general public problems has led to restrictions or outright bans on the growing of GM crops or their use in the production of food products in some parts of the world such as the European Union (EU). The basis of these concerns is that certain methods used to transfer the genes of modified DNA of a genetically modified plant are imprecise and unpredictable. This possibly may lead to unintended changes, such as differences in a food's nutritional values, toxic and allergic effects, lower crop yields, and unforeseen harm to the environment, that cannot be reversed (Legge Jr. and Durant 2010).

These factors mean the big multinationals have little incentive to develop GM crops for small or uncertain markets in developing nations or where poverty levels mean that farmers cannot afford to purchase GM seeds. As a consequence, farmers in developing nations are usually reliant upon GM plant research being undertaken in projects funded by their own governments. One such example is China where the government has funded research using rice genomic information to assist the conventional breeding process and directly applying genetic engineering technology to create new varieties. Successfully developed transgenic rice traits are insect- and disease-resistant aimed at overcoming the acute problems stemming from overuse of and/or heavy reliance on pesticides (Shen 2010).

Playbook Guideline 83: Technological entrepreneurship offers numerous opportunities to enhance agricultural productivity

Health Care

Shostak (2005) noted that since midway through the 20th century, the major multinational pharmaceutical companies have been very successful in developing small molecules that affect specific targets such as proteins or cells. In the small molecules model of drug development, a new formula is synthesized and tested in animal models and in clinical studies on human subjects. However, over the last two decades, there has been a growing interest in new forms of therapies based on stem cell technologies, biologics (i.e., larger molecules or aggregates of molecules), and the creation of new antibodies. The potential for these new forms of therapies is anchored in the understanding of the human genome. Skostak concluded, however, that the initial enthusiasm for the potential to develop therapies based on gene sequencing has been muted, reflecting the fact that identifying a connection between gene sequences and a specific medical disorder is a complex process.

Nevertheless, a new situation has emerged in the health care industry. This is because there has been a significant decline in the marginal return on investment in small molecule R&D, and the pharmaceutical industry has been forced to consider changes. Approaches such as new techno-scientific procedures involving stem cells, antibody, or biologics therapies are becoming established as complements to the small molecule therapies (Prainsack et al. 2008).

Understanding of the human genome has made valuable contributions to science, but produced only limited number of new therapies. Stem cell research is arguably capable of providing both new experimental methods and new forms of therapies in which cells are grown to replace poorly functioning or badly damaged cells in organs such as the eye or the liver. This and other areas of techno-scientific procedures have resulted in a shift in focus from "wet biology," wherein in-vivo studies are increasingly substituted by bio-computation, and bio-informatics models describing biological systems are simulated using software tools (Thacker 2006).

Genome sequencing has enabled modern biomedical research to relate more and more events in healthy as well as disease-affected cells and tissues to genomic sequences. The aim of "functional genomics" is to turn the huge amount of data obtained by observation and experiments into knowledge about life and life functions, with a focus on how genomic sequences determine normal and abnormal cell functioning. As more genome sequencing projects are undertaken, this fuels more and more projects in the area of functional genomics.

A major focus in functional genomics is to build upon the knowledge that errors in gene sequencing in DNA or RNA can lead to mutations. Identification of errors in gene sequences provides the basis for knowledge that can permit identification of the possible causes behind certain medical conditions such as cancers. This understanding can provide the basis for undertaking gene splicing. This involves manipulation of the gene sequence to create a change in the behavior of a specific type of cell, which when re-introduced into the patient can lead to effective treatment of an identified medical condition (Werner 2010).

Playbook Guideline 84: Technological entrepreneurship in the areas of DNA and RNA sequencing has the potential to revolutionize future medical treatments

Understanding Status

Case Aims: To illustrate how questions remain to be answered as an emerging area of technology comes into being

"Stem cells" is a term used to describe undifferentiated cells that are capable of indefinite self-renewal and have the potential to form other cells. These cells are medically valuable because of their ability to generate new cells and also many different types of cells. It is currently unclear whether the stem cells themselves promote regeneration or whether it is the factors released by the transplanted stem cells that are the real source of their regenerative effects (Smith 2009).

Smith described the role of stem cells is in replacing and repairing damaged cells and organs of the body. This is why the technology has attracted widespread interest often being seen as being at the forefront of hopes for future medical treatments for a range of debilitating and life-threatening human conditions. However, she noted that it is not easy to definitely confirm which diseases are actually already being successfully treated with stem cells, and in many cases, claims over miracle cures remain within the field speculation of scientists, journalists, and politicians.

One of the most widely known current therapeutic use of stem cells is the bone marrow transplant to treat leukemia and other blood disorders, including sickle cell anemia. These types of diseases are also currently treated with peripheral (adult) blood and umbilical cord blood stem cell transplants. Umbilical cord transplants have recently been reported as more successful at treating childhood leukemia than the standard treatment of bone marrow replacement. Where adult stem cell transplants have been attempted there is anecdotal evidence of clinical trial success in humans and in preclinical trials using animal. Nevertheless, there remains the need for more verifiable human clinical trial data in relation to the treatment of various neurological conditions, heart disease, spinal injuries, and certain autoimmune diseases. Stem cells also present hope for improved treatments and potentially cures either by transplanting or through research discovering and replicating the factors released by stem cells in repairing and regenerating cells for diseases as diverse as Parkinson's, osteoporosis, Alzheimer's, Type I Diabetes, and Motor Neuron Disease.

Robots

Twentieth-century science fiction writers have been extremely successful in describing new technology that has subsequently become reality. One area of such writings has been in relation to robots. These machines first appeared in real life in manufacturing environments such as car assembly plants. Their expansion into other roles was delayed, however, due to the need for advances in areas such as microchip memory storage capacity, more powerful software programs, and use of Artificial Intelligence (AI). These requirements are now being met, and as a consequence, robots now represent an area where emerging technology is resulting in machines offering significant potential as aids to human kind in a diversity of roles (Bibel 2014).

One important constraint in the process of developing more effective robots is these machines have tended to be solitary creatures, carrying out their allotted tasks with a single-minded purpose. This reflected by the fact that to-date, most robotics research has focused on building individual, autonomous machines. However, the era of the lone robot may be drawing to a close. This is because researchers have started to explore the possibilities of social machines capable of working together with minimal human supervision. In theory, collaborative robots hold enormous potential. They could augment human workers in high-risk situations such as firefighting or search and rescue or boost productivity in construction and manufacturing (Wright 2012).

A priority area of development is in using robots in the health care sector. This emphasis reflects factors such as the growing need to stabilize the costs of caring for the elderly in the face of population is aging, patient surgery, and patient recovery while in hospital. In relation to caregiving, researchers are developing social robotics to supplement or even replace human caregivers. These personal robots are created to act in any residential premise, such as at home and in nursing homes. Over time, robot carers can be expected to become part of standard health care service provision (Kachouie et al. 2014).

Robots designed as caregivers are required to have the ability to interact like humans with their patients. Robots for elderly people can be broadly categorized into two groups (Carrera et al. 2011). One group is the "rehabilitation robots" that focus on physical assistive technology and are principally not communicative. Examples include smart wheelchairs, advanced artificial limbs, and exoskeletons. The second group is "assistive social robots" that can be divided into two subgroups, namely service robots and companion robots. Service robots are used to support basic tasks of independent living, such as eating and bathing, mobility, navigation, or patient monitoring.

Another area attracting interest is enhancing safety and improved medical outcomes from surgical treatments. A recognized aspect of surgical treatments is that errors do occur within the operating theater. Causes of such errors include team instability due to lack of familiarity between nurses and surgeons, a lack of resources, distractions, and poor communi-cation. These factors increase the likelihood of instrument-count discrep-ancies caused by retention of surgical instruments in a patient's body along with disposables, such as sponges and towels, most common. Robotic scrub nurses under development are able to deliver surgical instruments to the surgeon by being able to understand the hand gestures and verbal requests from humans. These robots can also reduce the possibility of sur-gical instruments being retained within the patient's body by undertaking an accurate, thorough, and timely tracking of instruments in use during the operation (Mithun et al. 2013).

Robots are also perceived as having an important role in the trans-portation sector. Driverless trains have been in use for some years to link passenger terminals in a number of the world's airports. This is a relatively simple environment because the train is moving along a fixed track, and intervention, when necessary, can be based on using simple automated signaling systems. Once the concept of the driverless vehicle is extended to roads, the technological problems in areas such navigation, data collection, and decision making, become significantly much more complex. It was the highly entrepreneurial Google Corporation that decided to embark on the years of research to validate the viability of the driverless car. Having fully validated the technology, the car industry is finally accepting the market potential for the driverless car and is either investing in their own research projects or forming technological partnerships with high-tech companies such as Apple and Google. This growing interest has also prompted expanding the focus of robotic transportation systems to include other vehicles such as trucks and construction equipment (Blau 2015).

Playbook Guideline 85: Robotics offer the technological entrepreneur numerous new opportunities across a diversity of public and private sector scenarios

AI

In 1950, the British academic Alan Turing proposed that a machine's abil-ity to exhibit intelligent behavior could be tested to determine whether the activities of the machine are indistinguishable from that of a human

(Muggleton 2014). The ability of a machine to exhibit intelligence has since become known as AI. Machines utilizing AI are able to competently perform or mimic the cognitive functions that traditionally have been associated with humans. Modern examples of AI include computers that can beat professional players at games such as Chess and Go and self-driving cars.

Autor et al. (2006) opined that one possible impact as computer technologies such as AI spread across developed economies is employment opportunities will be clustered at the top of the market based around high-wage or high-education jobs and at the bottom in low-wage jobs requiring little education. Nevertheless, lower-skilled jobs such as those in retailing are also likely to be impacted. Already self-service checkout lanes in supermarkets are becoming increasingly common and with mobile apps available to support all aspects of the product purchase decision. This situation implies that the need for staff in terrestrial outlets may, over time, be reduced.

Ford (2015) noted that, in the past, many low-wage jobs have been protected from automation because humans are extremely good at tasks requiring mobility, dexterity, and hand–eye coordination. However, these advantages can be expected to diminish as more affordable robots utilizing AI software become available, which can mimic humans in the fulfillment of various job roles. It is unlikely that ongoing advances in AI will lead to immediate job destruction and rapidly rising unemployment. Nevertheless, as with the two previous Industrial Revolutions, in the current third Industrial Revolution, the structure and nature of job markets will change with opportunities in some sectors significantly diminished, while hopefully new opportunities will arise elsewhere within nations' economies.

Playbook Guideline 86: AI offers the technological entrepreneur numerous new opportunities across a diversity of public and private sector scenarios

The Internet of Things

The British entrepreneur Kevin Ashton is attributed to have coined the term the "Internet of Things" (or IoT). This area of technology is an open and partially standardized technological infrastructure that consists of unique identification devices (e.g., radio frequency identification or RFID devices) and sensors (e.g., to assess temperature, location, and vibration) embedded in everyday objects. These everyday objects are, in turn, embedded in a larger computer network and are often connected to servers and combined with other existing technologies in a modular manner. Data are communicated wirelessly. Taken together, IoT can be seen as distinctively different from the PC paradigm. This is because computing capabilities are not restricted to servers, fixed PCs, and laptops, but instead are distributed across devices embedded in everyday objects (Boos et al. 2013).

IoT offers the potential to improve activities in areas such as control of household appliances, supply chain management, health and safety management, and in retailing. In the case of retailing, IoT offers the potential for improved stock and asset management, reduced materials handling, greater information sharing, and better product tracking (Bose 2009). The retail example illustrates that most current IoT applications are mainly seen as allowing automation of data capture, thereby making manual intervention in data capture unnecessary. Within the supply chain, IoT technologies make it possible to automatically scan goods entering a warehouse and to update the information stored in a management information system in real time. This again results in the intervention of human actors becoming unnecessary. Some IoT applications can not only take over existing activities, but are also capable of supporting new functions, such as the complete and more accurate monitoring of the transportation path of goods (Bendavid and Cassivi 2010).

Playbook Guideline 87: IoT offers the technological entrepreneur numerous new opportunities across a diversity of public and private sector scenarios

Wearables

Case Aims: To illustrate how the exploitation of wearable IoT systems offers new entrepreneurial opportunities

One area of the IoT that is growing in importance is that of "wearable technology" such as that provided by smartwatches. These are worn by the user, and similar to the smartphone through exploitation of GPS, permit automatic identification of location. As well as functioning as a timekeeper, the smartwatch is typically in constant contact with its owner. This provides the capability of recognizing its owner's physical activities and location. In contrast, a limitation associated with smartphones is when users are not holding them, they cannot recognize any aspect of the users' physical or physiological condition. As a consequence, along with other forms of wearable technology, the smartwatch's continual connection to the skin offers new potential to revolutionize the provision of mobile health (or m-Health) provision. Software and hardware suppliers have already recognized the huge potential for the provision of new online entrepreneurial services. The location on the body of the smartwatch also permits easy recording of heart rate, heart rate variability, temperature, blood oxygen, and galvanic skin response (GSR). The latter attribute can be used to identify physiological arousal, especially when combined with heart rate and heart rate variability, with the potential to assess the emotional state of the wearer (Rawassizadeh et al. 2015).

References

Agarwal, R., M.B. Sarkar, and R. Echambadi. 2002. "The Conditioning Effect of Time on Firm Survival: An Industry Life Cycle Approach." *Academy of Management Journal* 45, no. 5, pp. 971–94.

Ahuja, M.K., D.F. Galletta, and K.M. Carley. 2003. "Individual Centrality and Performance in Virtual R&D Groups: An Empirical Study." *Management Science* 49, no. 1, pp. 21–38.

Allen, F., J. McAndres, and P. Strahan. 2002. "E-finance: An Introduction." *Journal of Financial Services Research* 22, no. 1/2, pp. 5–28.

Alvarez, S. and J. Barney. 2007. "Discovery and Creation: Alternative Theories of Entrepreneurial Action." *Strategic Entrepreneurship Journal* 1, no. 1, pp. 11–26.

Arman, H., and J. Foden. 2010. "Combining Methods in the Technology Intelligence Process: Application in an Aerospace Manufacturing Firm." *R&D Management* 40, no. 2, pp. 181–92.

Anderson, K. 1992. "The Purpose at the Heart of Management." *Harvard Business Review*, pp. 31–39.

Anderson, P., and M. Tushman. 1990. "Technological Discontinuities and Dominant Designs: A Cyclical Model of Technological Change." *Administrative Science Quarterly* 35, no. 4, pp. 604–33.

Anon. 2013. "The Secrets of Bezos." *Business Week*, pp. 58–76.

Anon. 2005. "Business Heroes–Ray Kroc." *Business Strategy Review* 16, no. 4, pp. 47–48.

Anon. 2006. "Workshop on Discontinuous Innovation." In *The 2nd JET International Technology and Innovation Conference*. London: The Institution of Engineering and Technology.

Anon. 2010. "It's a smart world." *The Economist*, pp. 3–24.

Anon. 2016. "Pump it up Scotty." *The Economist*, pp. 67–68.

Arbore, A., R. Graziani, and S. Venturini. 2014. "Understanding Personal Mobile Technologies: Decomposing and De-averaging the Value of a Smartphone." *Journal of Information Systems* 28, no. 1, pp. 167–85.

Ashcroft, B., D. Holden, and K. Low. 2009. "Entrepreneurial Interest, Vision and the Self-Employment Choice Decision in UK Regions." *Regional Studies* 43, no. 8, pp. 1075–90.

Augsdorfer, P. 2008. "Managing the Unmanageable." *Research Technology Management*, pp. 23–34.

Autor, D.H., L.F. Katz, and M.S. Kearney. 2006. "The Polarization of the US Labor Market." *American Economic Review* 96, no. 2, pp. 189–94.

Babarinsa, O.B., ed. 2011. "Technology Discontinuity as Motivation for Corporate Alliances." *SAM Advanced Management Journal*, pp. 4–11.

Baldwin, T. 2015. "The Trouble with Fonterra." *The New Zealand Herald*, pp. 12–13.

Bandura, A., ed. 1997. *Self-Efficacy: The Exercise of Control*. New York: Freeman.

Bannister, F., and D. Wilson. 2011. "Over-government?: Emerging Technology, Citizen Autonomy and the Regulatory State." *Information Polity* 16, pp. 63–79.

Barrett, M., E. Davidson, J. Prabhu, and S. Vargo. 2015. "Service Innovations in the Digital Age." *MIS Quarterly* 39, no. 1, pp. 135–56.

Beamish, P.W. 1999. "Sony's Yoshihide Nakamura on Structure and Decision Making." *Academy of Management Executive* 13, no. 4, pp. 2–16.

Beason, R., and D. Weinstein. 1995. "The MITI Myth." *American Enterprise* 6, no. 4, pp. 84–87.

Bendavid, Y., and L. Cassivi. 2010. "Bridging the Gap Between RFID/EPC Concepts, Technological Requirements and Supply Chain e-Business Processes." *Journal of Theoretical and Applied Electronic Commerce Research* 5, no. 3, pp. 1–16.

Benner, M.J., and M.L. Tushman. 2003. "Exploitation, Exploration, and Process Management: The Productivity Dilemma Revisited." *Academy of Management Review* 28, no. 2, pp. 38–56.

Bercovici, J., ed. 2014. "Move Over, Glass: With Oculus Acquisition, Facebook Out-Googles Google." New York, NY: Forbes.

Berwick, D.M. 2002. "A User's Manual for the IOM's "Quality Chasm" Report." *Health Affairs* 21, no. 3, pp. 80–90.

Bhattacharjee, S.M., R.D. Gopal, J.R. Marsden, and R. Sankaranayanan. 2009. "Re-tuning the Music Industry—Can They Re-attain Business Resonance?" *Communications of the ACM* 52, no. 6, pp. 136–50.

Bibel, W. 2014. "Artificial Intelligence in a Historical Perspective." *AI Communications* 27, no. 1, pp. 87–102.

Binshan, L., and D. Union. 2002. "e-healthcare; A Vehicle of Change." *American Business Review* 20, no. 2, pp. 47–55.

Birkinshaw, J., and C.B. Gibson. 2004. "Building Ambidexterity into an Organization." *Sloan Management Review* 45, no. 4, pp. 47–55.

Bisham, L., and D. Union. 2002. "E-Healthcare; A vehicle of Change." *American Business Review* 20, no. 2, pp. 47–55.

Blau, J. 2015. "Apple and Google Hope to Slide into the Driver's Seat." *Research-Technology Management*, pp. 3–7.

Blauth, M., R. Mauer, and M. Brettel. 2014. "Fostering Creativity in New Product Development Through Entrepreneurial Decision Making." *Creativity and Innovation Management* 23, no. 4, pp. 496–511.

Blomqvist, K., and J. Levy. 2006. "Collaboration Capability–A Focal Concept in Knowledge Creation and Collaborative Innovation in Networks." *International Journal of Management Concepts and Philosophy* 2, pp. 31–48.

Boos, D., H. Guenter, G. Grote, and K. Kinder. 2013. "Controllable Accountabilities: the Internet of Things and its Challenges for Organisations." *Behaviour and Information Technology* 32, no. 5, pp. 449–67.

Borman, S., ed. 1998. "Pharma Acquisitions." *Chemical and Engineering News*, London, pp. 47–67.

Bose, I.S. 2009. "Managing RFID Projects in Organizations." *European Journal of Information Systems* 18, no. 6, pp. 534–40.

Brown, B. 2007. "The Number of Online Personal Health Records Is Growing, but Is the Data in These Records Adequately Protected?" *Journal of Health Care Compliance*, pp. 60–65.

Brown, B., and M. Flynn. 2008. "The Meta-Trend Stakeholder Profile: The Changing Profile of Stakeholders in a Climate-and Water-Stressed World." *Greenfield Publishing* 54, pp. 37–46. Retrieved from www.greenfield-publishing.com

Brown, N., and S. Beynon-Jones. 2012. "Reflex Regulation: An Anatomy of Promissory Science Governance." *Health, Risk and Society* 14, no. 3, pp. 223–40.

Brueller, N.R., A. Carmeli, and I. Drori. 2014 "How Do Different Types of Mergers and Acquisitions Facilitate Strategic Agility?" *California Management Review* 56, no. 3, pp. 39–49.

Bughin, J., M. Chui, and J. Manyika. 2010. "Clouds, Big Data, and Smart Assets: Ten Tech-Enabled Business Trends to Watch." *McKinsey Quarterly* 56, no. 1, pp. 26–43.

Burgelman, R., C. Christensen, and S. Wheelwright. 2008. *Strategic Management of Technology and Innovation*. NewYork, NY: McGraw Hill.

Burgelman, R.A., and W. McKinney. 2006. "Acquisition Integration: Lessons from HP and Compaq." *California Management Review* 48, no. 1, pp. 6–14.

Burgelman, R.A., and R.A. Siegel. 2008. "Cutting the Strategy Diamond in High-Technology Ventures." *California Management Review* 50, no. 3, pp. 140–64.

Calof, J., and J. Smith. 2009. "The Integrative Domain of Foresight and Competitive Intelligence and its Impact on R&D Management." *R&D Management* 40, no. 1, pp. 31–40.

Carmeli, A., and B. Azerual. 2009. "How Relational Capital and Knowledge Combination Capability Enhance the Performance of Knowledge Work Units in a High-Technology Industry." *Strategic Entrepreneurship Journal* 3, no. 1, pp. 85–103.

Carrera, I., H. Moreno, R. Saltarén, C. Pérez, L. Puglisi, and C. Garcia. 2011. "ROAD: Domestic Assistant and Rehabilitation robot." *Medical & Biological Engineering & Computing* 49, no. 10, pp. 1201–11.

Chambers, J. 2015. "How We Did It." *Harvard Business Review*, pp. 35–40.

Chandy, R.K., and G.J. Tellis. 1998. "Organizing for Radical Product Innovation: The Overlooked Role of Willingness to Cannibalize." *Journal of Marketing Research* 35, no. 4, pp. 474–87.

Chao, R.O., and S. Kavadias. 2008. "A Theoretical Framework for Managing the New Product Development Portfolio: When and How to Use Strategic Buckets." *Management Science* 54, no. 5, pp. 907–21.

Chari, S., S. Katsikeas, G. Balabanis, and M. Robson. 2014. "Emergent Marketing Strategies and Performance: The Effects of Market Uncertainty and Strategic Feedback Systems." *British Journal of Management* 25, no. 2, pp. 145–65.

Chaston, I., ed. 2004. *Knowledge-Based Marketing*. London: Sage.

Chaston, I., ed. 2009a. *Entrepreneurship and Small Firms*. London: Sage.

Chaston, I., ed. 2009b. *Boomer Marketing: Exploiting a Recession Resistant Consumer Group*. Hampshire: Routledge.

Chaston, I., 2011. "Entrepreneurship and Knowledge Management in Small Service Sector Firms." *Service Industries Journal* 30, no. 1, pp. 23–32.

Chaston, I., ed. 2013. *Entrepreneurship and Innovation During Austerity*. London: Palgrave Macmillan.

Chaston, I., ed. 2014. *Small Business Marketing*, 2nd ed. London: Palgrave Macmillan.

Chaston, I., ed. 2015. *Internet Marketing and Big Data*. London: Palgrave MacMillan.

Chaston, I., ed. 2016. *Entrepreneurial Marketing*, 2nd ed. London: Palgrave Macmillan.

Chaston, I., and E. Sadler-Smith. 2012. "Entrepreneurial Cognition, Entrepreneurial Orientation and Firm Capability in the Creative Industries." *British Journal of Management* 23, pp. 415–32.

Chelariu, C., W.J. Johnston, and L. Young. 2002. "Learning to Improvise, Improvising to Learn: A Process of Responding to Complex Environments." *Journal of Business Research* 55, no. 2, pp. 141–47.

Chell, E., J. Haworthy, and S. Brearley. 1991. *The Entrepreneurial Personality*. London: Routledge.

Chen, C., P. Greene, and A. Crick. 1998. "Does Entrepreneurial Self-Efficacy Distinguish Entrepreneurs from Managers?" *Journal of Business Venturing* 13, pp. 295–316.

Chen, M. 2007. "Entrepreneurial Leadership and New Ventures: Creativity in Entrepreneurial Teams." *Creativity and Innovation Management* 16, no. 3, pp. 239–49.

Chesbrough, H. 2003. *Open Innovation: The New Imperative for Creating and Profiting from Technology*. Boston: Harvard Business School Press.

Chesbrough, H. 2010. "Business Model Innovation: Opportunities and Barriers." *Long Range Planning* 43, no. 2, pp. 354–63.

Chesbrough, H., and A.K. Crowther. 2006. "Beyond High-Tech: Early Adopters of Open Innovation in Other Industries." *R&D Management* 36, no. 3, pp. 229–36.

Christensen, C. 1997. *The Innovator's Dilemma.* Boston: Harvard Business School Press.

Christensen, C.M., S.D. Anthony, and E.A. Roth. 2004. *Seeing What's Next.* Boston: Harvard Business School Press.

Christensen, C.M., and M. Overdorf. 2000. "Meeting the Challenge of Disruptive Change." *Harvard Business Review* 78, no. 2, pp. 66–73.

Cockburn, I.M., R. Henderson, and S. Stern. 2000. "Untangling the Origins of Competitive Advantage." *Strategic Management Journal* 21, no. 10/11, pp. 1123–45.

Cohen, S. 2015. "What is Stopping the Renewable Energy Transformation and What Can the US Government Do?" *Social Research* 82, no. 3, pp. 689–98.

Colarelli, D., G.O'Connor, and R. DeMartino. 2006. "Organizing for Radical Innovation: An Exploratory Study of Structural Aspects of RI Management Systems in Large Established Organisations." *European Journal of Work and Organizational Psychology* 8, no. 1, pp. 9–32.

Collins, M.A., and T.M. Amabile. 1999. "Motivation and Creativity." In *Handbook of creativity*, ed. R.J. Sternberg, 46–59. Cambridge: Cambridge University Press.

Conger, J. 1999. "The Dark Side of Leadership." *Organisational Dynamics* 14, pp. 43–55.

Cooper, R.G. 2011. "Perspective: The Innovation Dilemma: How to Innovate When the Market is Mature." *Journal of Product Innovation Management* 28, no. 1, pp. 2–27.

Cooper, R.G., S. Edgett, and E.J. Kleinschmidt. 1997. "Portfolio Management in New Product Development: Lessons from the Leaders." *Research Technology Management* 40, no. 6, pp. 43–53.

Cooper, R.G., S.J. Edgett, and E.J. Kleinschmidt. 2004. "Benchmarking Best NPD Practices." *Research Technology Management* 47, no. 1, pp. 31–43.

Covin, D., and J. Slevin. 1990. "Judging Entrepreneurial Style and Organizational Structure: How to Get Your Act Together." *Sloan Management Review* 31, no. 4, pp. 45–56.

Covin, J.G., K. Green, and D. Slevin. 2006. "Strategic Process Effects on the Entrepreneurial Orientation–Sales Growth Rate Relationship." *Entrepreneurship Theory and Practice* 30, pp. 57–81.

Coyne, W.E. 2001. "How 3M Innovates for Long-Term Growth." *Research and Technology Management*, pp. 54–63.

Coyne, K.R., S.D. Hall, and P.G. Clifford. 1997. "Is Your Competence a Mirage?" *The McKinsey Quarterly* 1, pp. 40–47.

Cunhae, M.P. 2007. "Entrepreneurship as Decision Making: Rational, Intuitive and Improvisational Approaches." *Journal of Enterprising Culture* 15, no. 1, pp. 1–20.

Cusumano, M.A. 2015. "Technology Strategy and Management: How Traditional Firms Must Compete in the Sharing Economy." *Communications of the ACM* 58, no. 1, pp. 32–33.

Danes, S.M. 2013. "Entrepreneurship Success: "The Lone Ranger" versus "It Takes a Village" Approach?" *Entrepreneurship Research Journal* 3, no. 3, pp. 277–85.

Darling, J.R., and S.A. Beebe. 2007. "Effective Entrepreneurial Communication in Organization Development: Achieving Excellence Based on Leadership Strategies and Values." *Organization Development Journal* 25, no. 1, pp. 71–83.

Dascher, E.D., J. Kang, and G. Hustvedt. 2014. "Water Sustainability: Environmental Attitude, Drought Attitude and Motivation." *International Journal of Consumer Studies* 38, no. 5, pp. 467–74.

Datta, A., D. Mukherjee, and L. Jessup. 2015. "Understanding Commercialization of Technological Innovation: Taking Stock and Moving Forward." *R&D Management* 45, no. 3, pp. 240–51.

David, A. 1995. "The Role of Behavioural Formality and Informality." *Academy of Management Review* 20, no. 4, pp. 831–72.

David, P., and J. Bunn. 1988. "The Economics of Gateway Technologies and Network Evolution." *Information Economics and Policy* 3, pp. 165–202.

Day, D.L. 1994. "Raising Radicals." *Organization Science* 5, pp. 148–172.

Day, G.S., and P.J.H. Schoemaker. 2005. "Scanning the Periphery." *Harvard Business Review* 83, no. 11, pp. 135–146.

De Haan, A., and K. Mulder. 2002. "Sustainable Air Transport: In Possibilities for Technological Regime Shifts in Aircraft Construction." *Journal of Innovation Management* 6, no. 3, pp. 301–18.

De Liu, R., W. Gautam, and B. Andrew. 2010. "The Interaction Between Knowledge Codification and Knowledge-Sharing Networks." *Information Systems Research* 21, no. 4, pp. 892–906.

Dedrick, J., and K.L. Kraemer. 2006. "Is Production Pulling Knowledge Work to China? A Study of the Notebook PC Industry." *IEEE Computer* 39, no. 7, pp. 36–42.

den Uijl, S., and H.J. de Vries. 2013. "Pushing Technological Progress by Strategic Manoeuvring: the Triumph of Blu-ray Over HD-DVD." *Business History* 55, no. 8, pp. 1361–84.

Dess, G., G.T. Lumpkin, and J.G. Covin. 1997. "Entrepreneurial Strategy Making and Firm Performance: Tests of Contingency and Configuration Models." *Strategic Management Journal* 18, no. 9, pp. 677–95.

Dess, G.G., R.D. Ireland, S.A. Zahra, S.W. Floyd, J.J. Janney, and P.J. Lane. 2003. "Emerging Issues in Corporate Entrepreneurship." *Journal of Management* 29, no. 2, pp. 351–78.

DiBella, A.J. 1995. "Developing Learning Organizations: a Matter of Perspective." *Academy of Management Journal, Best Papers Proceedings*, pp. 287–290.

Dmitriev, V., G. Simmons, Y. Truong, M. Palmer, and D. Schneckenberg. 2014. "An Exploration of Business Model Development in the Commercialization of Technology Innovations." *R&D Management* 44, no. 3, pp. 305–16.

Dorobaț, C.A. 2014. "Jean-Baptiste Say: Revolutionary, Entrepreneur, Economist." *Quarterly Journal of Austrian Economics* 17, no. 1, pp. 112–16.

Doz, Y., and M. Kosonen. 2008. "The Dynamics of Strategic Agility: Nokia's Rollercoaster Experience." *California Management Review* 50, no. 3, pp. 95–118.

Dubini, P., and H. Aldrich. 1991. "Personal and Extended Networks are Central to the Entrepreneurial Process." *Journal of Business Venturing* 8, no. 3, pp. 27–38.

Duhigg, C., and I. Bradsher. 2012. "How the U.S. Lost Out on iPhone Work." *The New York Times* 21.

Durant, R.F. 2010. "Public Opinion, Risk Assessment, and Biotechnology: Lessons from Attitudes Toward Genetically Modified Foods in the European Union." *Review of Policy Research* 27, no. 1, pp. 59–76.

Edelman, L., and H. Yli-Renko. 2010. "The Impact of Environment and Entrepreneurial Perceptions on Venture-Creation Efforts." *Entrepreneurship Theory and Practice* 34, no. 5, pp. 833–41.

Ehrnberg, D., and N. Sjöberg. 1995. "Technological Discontinuities, Competition and Firm Performance." *Technological Strategic Management* 7, pp. 93–107.

Eisberg, N. 2015. "Wear IT well." *Chemistry & Industry*, pp. 32–36.

Elbanna, S., and J. Child. 2007. "The Influence of Decision, Environmental and Firm Characteristics on the Rationality of Strategic Decision-Making." *Journal of Management Studies* 44, pp. 561–91.

Embner, W.J., M. Leimester, and H. Krcmar. 2009. "Community Engineering for Innovation: The Ideas Competition for Nurturing a Virtual Community for Innovation." *Research Technology Management* 39, no. 4, pp. 345–56.

Engel, J.S., and I. del-Palacio. 2011. "Global Clusters of Innovation: The Case of Israel and Silicon Valley." *California Management Review* 53, no. 2, pp. 27–49.

Engel, J.S., and I. del-Palacio. 2015. "Global Clusters of Innovation: Lessons from Silicon Valley." *California Management Review* 57, no. 2, pp. 37–58.

Entine, J. 1995. "The Body Shop: Truth & Consequences." *DCI*, pp. 54–59.

Epstein, A.H. 2014. "Innovation and Value Creation in a Very Long-cycle Business." *Technology Management* 57, no. 6, pp. 21–25.

Evans, J., and R. Johnson. 2013. "Tools for Managing Early-Stage Business Model Innovation." *Research-Technology Management* 56, no. 5, pp. 52–61.

Farrington, T., K. Henson, and C. Crews. 2012. "Research Foresights." *Research Technology Management* 55, no. 2, pp. 26–33.

Feder, J., H. Komisar, and A. Niefeld. 2000. "Long Term Care in the United States: An Overview." *Health Affairs* 19, no. 3, pp. 40–56.

Fleming, L., and O. Sorenson. 2004. "Science as a Map in Technology Search." *Strategic Management Journal* 25, no. 8/9, pp. 909–28.

Forbes, D.P. 2005. "The Effects of Sstrategic Decision Making on Entrepreneurial Self-efficacy." *Entrepreneurship Theory and Practice* 29, pp. 599–612.

Ford, M. 2015. "Could Artificial Intelligence Create an Unemployment Crisis?" *Communications of the ACM* 56, no. 7, pp. 35–38.

Fottler, M.D., and R. Ford. 2002. "Creating Customer Focus," In *Human resources in healthcare: Managing for success*, eds. J. Fried and J.A. Johnson, 56–74. Washington, DC: AUPHA Press.

Fox, J. 2016. "Airbnb: How the Sharing Economy is Affecting New York City Hotels." *New York: Hotel Management*, pp. 90–92.

Fuchs, G., and G. Krauss. 2003. "Biotechnology in Comparative Perspective." In *Biotechnology in comparative perspective*, ed. G. Fuchs, 1–13. New York, NY: Routledge.

Gallaugher, T. 2010. "Challenging the Conventional Wisdom of Internet Strategies." *Communications of the ACM* 57, no. 7, pp. 27–36.

Gans, J., and S. Stern. 2004. *Managing Ideas: Commercialization Strategies for Biotechnology*. Chicago: Northwestern Academic Press.

Garner, R. 2005. "Post-It® Note Persuasion: A Sticky Influence." *Journal of Consumer Psychology* 15, no. 3, pp. 230–23.

Gehring, D.R. 2007. "Applying Traits Theory of Leadership Management to Project Management." *Project Management Journal* 38, no. 1, pp. 44–52.

Gemmell, R.M., R. Boland, and D. Kolb. 2011. "The Socio-Cognitive Dynamics of Entrepreneurial Ideation." *Entrepreneurship Theory and Practice* 23, pp. 1053–69.

Gertner, J. 2014. *The X factor*. 66–108. New York, NY: Fast Company.

Gevero, A., and E. Alves. 2015. "How Uber and Other Ride-Sharing Companies are Roiling the Taxi Medallion." *Risk Management Journal* 98, no. 4, pp. 36–41.

Ghoshal, S., and B. Barlett. 1995. "Changing the Role of Top Management: Beyond Structure to Processes." *Harvard Business Review*, pp. 4–11.

Giachetti, C., and G. Marchi. 2010. "'Evolution of Firms' Product Strategy Over the Life Cycle of Technology-Based Industries: A Case Study of the Global Mobile Phone Industry, 1980–2009." *Business History* 52, no. 7, pp. 1123–50.

Gilman, M., and J. Stensland. 2013. "Telehealth and Medicare: Payment Policy, Current Use, and Prospects for Growth." *Medicare & Medicaid Research Review* 3, no. 4, pp 1–14.

Glazer, R. 1999. "Winning in Smart Markets." *Sloan Management Review* 40, no. 4, pp. 59–69.

Goldsmith, M. 2010. "Five Classic Challenges for Entrepreneurial Leaders: Coaching and Mentoring Entrepreneurial Winners." In *Creating Entrepreneurs: Making Miracles Happen,* ed. F. Kiesner, Singapore: World Scientific.

Goyal, E., and S. Srivastava. 2015. "Study on Customer Engagement Models." *SIES Journal of Management* 11, no. 1, pp. 51–58.

Gray, J. 2016. "Dairy Doldrums Hit Farm Values." Business Section, The New Zealand Herald, Auckland, 18 March, p. 5.

Green, R. 2008. "Electricity Wholesale Markets: Designs Now and in a Low-Carbon Future." *Energy Journal* 29, no. 2, pp. 95–124.

Gregoire, D.A., and D.A. Shepherd. 2012. "Technology-Market Combinations and the Identification of Entrepreneurial Opportunities." *Academy of Management Journal* 55, no. 4, pp. 753–785.

Guimaraes, T., B. Bransford, and R. Guimaraes. 2010. "Empirically Testing Some Major Factors for Bank Innovation Success." *Journal of Performance Management* 14, no. 2, pp. 35–43.

Gupta, V., I.C. MacMillan, and G. Surie. 2004. "Entrepreneurial Leadership: Developing and Measuring a Cross-Cultural Construct." *Journal of Business Venturing* 19, no. 2, pp. 241–60.

Gupta, A.K., K.G. Smith, and C.E. Shalley. 2006. "The Interplay Between Exploration and Exploitation." *Academy of Management Journal* 49, no. 4, pp. 693–706.

Habtay, S.R. 2012. "A Firm-Level Analysis on the Relative Difference Between Technology-Driven and Market-Driven Disruptive Business Model Innovations." *Creativity and Innovation Management* 21, no. 3, pp. 291–302.

Haigh, T. 2012. "The IBM PC: From Beige Box to Industry Standard." *Communications of the ACM* 55, no. 1, pp. 35–37.

Hallier, J. 2004. "Embellishing the Past: Middle Manager Identity and Informality in the Implementation of New Technology." *New Technology, Work & Employment* 19, no. 1, pp. 43–62.

Hamal, G., and C. Pralahad. 1994. *Competing for the Future.* Harvard, MA: Harvard Business School Press.

Helm, B. 2012. "James Dyson, Inc." *Fortune Magaziner* 34, no. 2, pp. 74–76.

Helm, B., and M. Guzzetta. 2014. "Airbnb Company of the Year" *Inc. Magazine* 36, no. 10, pp. 64–68.

Helper, S., and P. Henderson. 2014. "Management Practices, Relational Contracts, and the Decline of General Motors." *Journal of Economic Perspectives* 28, no. 1, pp. 49–72.

Hervas-Oliver, J., and J. Albors-Garrigos. 2014. "Are Technology Gatekeepers Renewing Clusters? Understanding Gatekeepers and Their Dynamics Across Cluster Life Cycles." *Entrepreneurship & Regional Development* 26, no. 5/6, pp. 431–452.

Hill, C.W., and F.T. Rothaermel. 2003. "The Performance of Incumbent Firms in the Face of Radical Technological Innovation." *Academy of Management Review* 28, no. 2, pp. 257–274.

Hintz, E.S. 2016. "A Triumph of Genius: Edwin Land, Polaroid, and the Kodak Patent War." *Business History Review* 90, no. 1, pp. 131–133.

Hjorth, D. 2008. "Nordic Entrepreneurship Research." *Entrepreneurship: Theory & Practice* 32, no. 2, pp. 313–338.

Hoffmann, V.H., and T. Busch. 2008. "Corporate Carbon Performance Indicators." *Journal of Industrial Ecology* 12, no. 4, pp. 505–20.

Ho, S.K., and W.K. Cho. 1995. "Manufacturing Excellence in Fast-Food Chains." *Total Quality Management* 6, no. 2, pp 123–134.

Huet, E., and L. Chen. 2015. "World War Uber." *Forbes*, p. 2.

Hull, D., and J. Johnsson. 2016. "SpaceX Rocket Mission Turns Science Fiction into Reality." Auckland: The New Zealand Herald, pp. B5–B6.

IBM archives, at www-03.ibm.com/ibm/history/exhibits/pc25/pc25_birth.html (accessed November 10, 2015).

Ilies, R., D. Judge, and D. Wagner. 2006. "Making Sense of Motivational Leadership: The Trail from Transformational Leaders to Motivated Followers." Journal of Leadership & Organizational Studies.

Ireland, R.D., M.A. Hitt, and D.G. Sirmon. 2003. "A Model of Strategic Entrepreneurship: The Construct and Its Dimensions." *Journal of Management* 29, no. 6, pp. 963–989.

Isaacson, W. 2011. *Steve Jobs*. New York, NY: Simon & Schuster.

Jarratt, D., and D. Stiles.2010. "How Are Methodologies and Tools Framing Managers' Strategizing Practice in Competitive Strategy Development." *British Journal of Management* 21, pp. 28–43.

Jarvenpaa, S.L., and L. Välikangas. 2014. "Creation in Innovation Networks." *California Management Review* 57, no. 1, pp. 67–87.

Jorgensen, D.W., and M.P. Timmer. 2011. "Structural Change in Advanced Nations: A New Set of Stylised Facts." *Scandinavian Journal of Economics* 113, no. 11, pp. 1–29.

Kachouie, R., S. Sedighadeli, R. Khosla, and M. Chu. 2014. "Socially Assistive Robots in Elderly Care." *International Journal of Human–Computer Interaction* 30, pp. 369–393.

Kay, A. 2004. "Strategic Management, Core Competence and Flexibility: Learning Issues for Select Pharmaceutical Organizations." *Global Journal of Flexible Systems Management* 5, no. 4, pp. 1–15.

Kay, J.A. 1993. *Foundations of Corporate Success: How Business Strategies Add Value*. Oxford: Oxford University Press.

Kay, M. 2011. "Water Smart: The Role of Water and Technology in Food Security." *International Trade Forum* no. 3, pp. 24–25.

Kellermanns, F., J. Walter, T.R. Crook, B. Kemmerer, and V. Narayanan. 2016. "The Resource-Based View in Entrepreneurship: A Content-Analytical Comparison of Researchers' and Entrepreneurs' Views." *Journal of Small Business Management* 54, no. 1, pp. 26–48.

Kelly, N. 2010. "Corning's Promising and Very Profitable Future." *American Ceramic Society Bulletin* 87, no. 2, pp. 32–39.

Kets de Vries, M.E. 1985. "The Dark Side of Entrepreneurship." *Harvard Business Review*, pp. 160–171.

Key, P., and Y. Hufenbach. 2014. "Engineering the Value Network of the Customer Interface and Marketing in the Data-Rich Retail Environment." *International Journal of Electronic Commerce* 18, no. 4, pp. 17–42.

Khurana, A. 2006. "Strategies for Global R&D." *Research Technology Management*, pp. 5–14.

Kim, Y., B. Min, and J. Cha. 1999. "The Roles of R&D Team Leaders in Korea: A Contingent Approach." *R&D Management* 29, no. 2, pp. 153–65.

Kinden, S., K. Kraemer, and J. Dedrick. 2009. "Who Captures Value in a Global Innovation Network? The Case of Apple's iPod." *Communication of the ACM* 5, no. 3, pp. 140–145.

Kirzner, I.M. 1997. "Entrepreneurial Discovery and the Competitive Market Process: An Austrian approach." *Journal of Economic Literature* 35, no. 1, pp. 60–85.

Kirzner, J.M. 1973. *Competition and Entrepreneurship*. Chicago: University of Chicago Press.

Kisswani, K. 2015. "OPEC and Political Considerations When Deciding on Oil Extraction." *Journal of Economics & Finance* 39, no. 1, pp. 118–129.

Klein, J. 2002. "Beyond Competitive Advantage." *Strategic Change* 11, no. 6, pp. 317–327.

Kluger, J. 2012. "Rocket Man." *Time International* (South Pacific Edition), pp. 38–42.

Knapp, A. 2012. "NASA Awards Over $1 billion in Contracts to Develop Commercial Spaceflight." *Forbes*, p. 15.

Knapp, A. 2016. "SpaceX Launches Communications Satellite and Sticks Another Landing Knowledge-Based Approaches." *European Journal of Innovation Management* 5, no. 2, pp. 33–42.

Koen, P., H. Bertels, and I. Elsum. 2011. "The Three Faces of Business Model Innovation: Challenges for Established Firms." *Research Technology Management*, pp. 32–41.

Kolk, A., and J. Pinkse. 2005. "Business Responses to Climate Change: Emergent Strategies." *California Management Review* 47, no. 3, pp. 6–14.

Kollmann, T., and C. Stöckmann. 2014. "Filling the Entrepreneurial Orientation-Performance Gap: The Mediating Effects of Exploratory and Exploitative Innovations." *Entrepreneurship: Theory & Practice* 38, no. 5, pp. 1001–26.

Krueger, N., and D. Brazeal. 1994. "Entrepreneurial Potential and Potential Entrepreneurs." *Entrepreneurship Theory & Practice* 18, pp. 91–104.

Kuratko, D.F., R.V. Montagno, and J.S. Hornsby. 1990. "Developing an Intrapreneurial Assessment Instrument for an Effective Corporate Entrepreneurial Environment." *Strategic Management Journal* 11, pp. 49–58.

Lambe, C.J., and R.E. Spekman. 1997. "Alliances, External Technology Acquisition, and Discontinuous Technological Change." *Journal of Product Innovation Management* 14, no. 2, pp. 102–116.

Lanser, G. 2000. "Lessons from the Business Side of Healthcare." *Healthcare Executive*, pp. 14–19.

Lanterman, M. 2015. "Not What the Doctor Ordered: Security Concerns in Light of Evolving Health Technologies." *Journal of Health Care Compliance*, pp. 5–11.

LaPlante, A. 2007. "Compaq and HP: Ultimately, the Urge to Merge was Right." www.gsb.stanford.edu/insights/compaq-hp-ultimately-urge-merge-was-right (accessed May 2016).

Lashinsky, A., D. Burke, and J.P. Mangalindan. 2012. "Inside the Mind of Jeff Bezos." *Fortune*, pp. 100–103.

Lawton, T., and K. Michaels. 2001. "Advancing to the Virtual Value Chain: Learning from the Dell model." *Irish Journal of Management* 22, no. 1, pp. 91–113.

Lazzarotti, V., R. Manzini, and L. Pellegrini. 2010. "Open Innovation Models Adopted in Practice: An Extensive Study in Italy." *Business Excellence* 14, no. 4, pp. 11–23.

Legge, J.S., Jr., and R.F. Durant. 2010. "Public Opinion, Risk Assessment, and Biotechnology: Lessons from Attitudes Toward Genetically Modified Foods in the European Union." *Review of Policy Research* 27, no. 1, pp. 59–76.

Lett, C., C. Herstatt, and H.G. Gemuenden. 2006. "Users' Contributions to Radical Innovation: Evidence from Four Cases in the Field of Medical Equipment Technology." *R&D Management* 36, no. 3, pp. 251–268.

Lewis, M.W., M.A. Welsh, G. Dehler, and S. Green. 2002. "Product Development Tensions: Exploring Contrasting Styles of Project Management." *Academy of Management Journal* 45, no. 2, pp. 546–564.

Li, Q., P. Magitti, K. Smith, P. Tesluk, and R. Kahla. 2013. "Top Management and Attention to Innovation." *Academy of Management Journal* 56, no. 3, pp. 893–916.

Liao, J., H.P. Welsch, and D. Pistrui. 2001. "Environmental and Individuals Determinants of Entrepreneurial Growth: An Empirical Examination." *Journal of Enterprising Culture* 9, no. 3, pp. 253–273.

Lichtenthaler, E. 2004. "Technological Change and the Technology Intelligence Process: A Case Study." *Journal of Engineering and technology Management* 21, no. 4, pp. 331–348.

Lichtenthaler, U. 2009. "Outbound Open Innovation and Its Effect on Firm Performance: Examining Environmental Influences." *R&D Management* 39, no. 4, pp. 317–30.

Lin, Y., Y. Wang, and L. Kung. 2015. "Influences of Cross-Functional Collaboration and Knowledge Creation on Technology Commercialization: Evidence from High-Tech Industries." *Industrial Marketing Management* 49, pp. 128–138.

Lind, J. 2006. "Boeing's Global Enterprise Technology Process." *Technology Management* 49, no. 5, pp. 31–43.

Link, S. 2014. "Henry Ford." *Business History Review* 88, no. 2, pp. 397–399.

Lumpkin, G.T., and G.G. Dess. 1996. "Clarifying the Entrepreneurial Orientation Construct and Linking It to Performance." *Academy of Management Review* 21, no. 1, pp. 135–172.

Magrath, A.J. 1986. "When Marketing Services, 4 Ps are Not Enough." *Business Horizons* 29, no. 3, pp. 44–51.

Mahdi, A., A. Hussain, M. Abbas, T.I. Mazar, and G. Shaju. 2015. "A Comparative Analysis of Strategies and Business Models of Nike, Inc. and Adidas Group with Special Reference to Competitive Advantage in the Context of a Dynamic and Competitive Environment." *International Journal of Business Management & Economic Research* 6, no. 3, pp. 167–177.

March, J.G. 1991. "Exploration and Exploitation in Organizational Learning." *Organization Science* 2, pp. 71–87.

March, J.G. 1991. "Exploration and Exploitation in Organizational Learning." *Organization Science* 2, pp. 71–87.

Marion, T.J., and J.H. Friar. 2012. "Managing Global Outsourcing to Enhance Lean Innovation." *Research-Technology Management*, pp. 44–52.

Mayer, D.M., M.G. Erhart, and B. Schneider. 2009. "Service Attribute Boundary Conditions." *Academy of Management Journal* 52, no. 5, pp. 1034–50.

McCleary, K.J., P.A. Rivers, and E.S. Schneller. 2006. "A Diagnostic Approach to Understanding Entrepreneurship in Healthcare." *Journal of Health and Human Services Administration* 28, no. 4, pp. 550–562.

McGee, J.E., M. Peterson, S.L. Mueller, and J.M. Sequeira. 2009. "Entrepreneurial Self-Efficacy: Refining the Measure." *Entrepreneurship Theory and Practice* 33, no. 4, pp. 965–988.

McKelvey, S.M. 2006. "Coca-Cola vs. PepsiCo—A Super Battleground for the Cola Wars?" *Sport Marketing Quarterly* 15, no. 2, pp. 114–123.

Mehta, S.N., J. Schlosser, and P. Hjelt. 2001. "Cisco Fractures Its Own Fairy Tale." *Fortune Magazine* 143, no. 10, pp. 104–114.

Mehta, S.N. 2001. "Can Corning Find Its Optic Nerve?" *Fortune* 143, no. 6, pp. 148–150.

Metzner, D., and G. Reger. 2009. "Practices of Strategic Foresight in Biotech Companies." *International Journal of Innovation Management* 13, no. 2, pp. 273–294.

Miller, D. 1983. "The Correlates of Entrepreneurship in Three Types of Firm." *Management Science* 29, no. 7, pp. 770–782.

Millier, P., and R. Palmer. 2001. "Turning Innovation into Profit." *Strategic Change* 10, no. 2, pp. 87–98.

Mintzberg, H. 1990. "The Design School: Reconsidering the Basic Premises of Strategic Management." *Strategic Management Journal* 11, no. 3, pp. 171–195.

Mintzberg, H. 1999. "Reflecting on the Strategy Process." *Sloan Management Review* 40, no. 3, pp. 21–32.

Mintzberg, H., and F. Westley. 2001. "Decision Making: It's Not What You Think." *Sloan Management Review* 42, no. 3, pp. 89–93.

Mithun, G., Y. Li, G.A. Akingba, and J.P. Wachs. 2013. "Collaboration with a Robotic Scrub Nurse." *Communications of the ACM* 56, no. 5, pp. 23–29.

Moorman, C., and A.S. Miner. 1998. "The Convergence of Planning and Execution: Improvisation in New Product Development." *Journal of Marketing* 62, no. 3, pp. 1–20.

Morris, M., M. Schindehutte, and J. Allen. 2005. "The Entrepreneur's Business Model: Toward a Unified Perspective." Journal of Business Research 58, no. 6, pp. 726–735.

Muggleton, S. 2014. "Alan Turing and the Development of Artificial Intelligence." *AI Communications* 27, no. 1, pp. 3–10.

Müller, C., T. Fujiwara, and C. Herstatt. 2004. "Bio-Entrepreneurship in Germany and Japan." *Journal of Small Business Management* 42, no. 1, pp. 93–101.

Muller, J. 2015. How Badly Does Toyota Want to Push Hydrogen Cars? It's Giving Away Its Patents for Free, Forbes, New York, 5th January 2015, p. 30.

Murtaugh, D. 2016. "Shale Drillers Run Out of Places to Cut." *Business Week*, pp. 38–39.

Nambisan, S., and M. Sawhney. 2011. "Orchestration Processes in Network-Centric Innovation: Evidence from the Field." *Academy of Management Perspectives* 25, no. 3, pp. 40–57.

Narayanan, V.K. 2001. *Managing Technology and Innovation for Competitive Advantage.* New York, NY: Prentice-Hall.

Narula, R. 2004. "R&D Collaboration by SMEs: New Opportunities and Limitations in the Face of Globalisation." *Technovation* 24, no. 2, pp. 153–161.

Nuvolari, A., and B. Verspagen. 2009. "Technical Choice, Innovation, and British Steam Engineering." *Economic History Review* 62, no. 3, pp. 685–710.

O'Driscoll, A., D. Carson, and A. Gilmore. 2001. "The Competence Trap: Exploring Issues in Winning and Sustaining Core Competence." *Irish Journal of Management* 22, no. 1, pp. 73–90.

O'Connor, G.C., and M.P. Rice. 2013. *New Market Creation for Breakthrough Innovations: Manage What They Know.* Boston, MA: Harvard Business School Press.

O'Driscoll, C. 2012. "Smarter Irrigation Technology." Chemistry and Industry, p. 48.

O'Reilly, C., and M. Tushman. 2004. "The Ambidextrous Organization." *Harvard Business Review* 82, no. 4, pp. 74–81.

O'Reilly, C.A., and M.L. Tushman. 2011. "Organizational Ambidexterity in Action." *California Management Review* 53, no. 4, pp. 5–22.

O'Driscoll, A., D. Carson, and A. Gilmore. 2001. "The Competence Trap: Exploring Issues in Winning and Sustaining Core Competence." *Irish Journal of Management* 22, no. 1, pp. 73–90.

Ozanian, M.K. 1995, "Darkness Before Dawn." *Financial World*, pp. 42–46.

Parasuraman, A., V.A. Zeithaml, and L.B. Berry. 1988. "Servqual: Multiple-Item Scale for Measuring Consumer Perception of Service Quality." *Journal of Retailing* 64, no. 1, pp. 12–40.

Patrizi, P., T.E. Heid, J. Coffman, and T. Beer. 2013. "Eyes Wide Open: Learning as Strategy Under Conditions of Complexity and Uncertainty." *Foundation Review* 5, no. 3, pp. 50–65.

Phillip, F.S., and A.N. Garman. 2006. "Barriers to Entrepreneurship in Healthcare Organisations." *Journal of Health and Human Services Administration* 28, no. 4, pp. 471–486.

Piccoli, G., M.K. Brohman, R.T. Watson, and A. Parasuraman. 2004. "Net-Based Customer Service Systems: Evolution and Revolution in Web Site Functionalities." *Decision Science* 35, no. 3, pp. 423–455.

Piercy, N.F., D.W. Cravens, and N. Lane. 2010. "Marketing Out of the Recession: Recovery Is Coming, But Things Will Never be the Same Again." *Marketing Review* 10, no. 1, pp. 3–23.

Porter, M. 1980. *Industry and Competitive Advantage.* New York, NY: Free Press.

Porter, M.E. 1985. *Competitive Advantage.* New York, NY: The Free Press.

Prainsack, B., I. Gesink, and S. Franklin. 2008. "Stem Cell Technologies 1998–2008: Controversies and Silences." *Science as Culture* 17, pp. 351–362.

Pyka, A. 2002. "Innovation Networks in Economics: from the Incentive-Based to the Knowledge-Based Approaches." *European Journal of Innovation Management* 5, no. 3, pp. 152–63.

PWC (PricewaterhouseCoopers). 2008. MoneyTree™ Report. www.pwcmoneytree.com/MTPublic (accessed May 2016).

Qaim, M. 2005. "Agricultural Biotechnology Adoption in Developing Countries." *American Journal of Agricultural Economics* 87, no. 5, pp. 1317–24.

Radjou, A., J. Prabhu, and S. Ahuja. 2012. *Jugaad innovation*. San Francisco, CA: Jossey-Bass.

Rae, J. 2007. "Debate: Six Sigma vs. Innovation." *Business Week*, pp. 3–6.

Raich, M., and M. Crepaz. 2009. "Fitting New Brand Principles: First Encounter at Bank Branches." *Journal of Brand Management* 16, no. 7, pp. 480–91.

Rapp, W.V. 2007. "Hydrocarbons to Hydrogen Toyota's Long-Term IT-Based Smart Product Strategy." *The Business Review* 7, no. 2, pp. 1–7.

Rawassizadeh, R., B.L. Price, and M. Petre. 2015. "Wearables: Has the Age of Smartwatches Finally Arrived?" *Communications of the ACM* 58, no. 1, pp. 45–49.

Reinke, T. 2015. "Leading Health Systems Switch Focus from Genetics to Genomes." *Physician Leadership Journal Advances* 2, no. 2, pp. 29–34.

Riva, G. 2000. "From Telehealth to e-health: Internet and Distributed Virtual Reality in Health Care." *CyberPsychology & Behavior* 3, no. 6, pp. 989–98.

Rost, K. 2011. "The Strength of Strong Ties in the Creation of Innovation." *Research Policy* 40, no. 4, pp. 588–604.

Rothaermel, F.T. 2001. "Complementary Assets, Strategic Alliances, and the Incumbent's Advantage: An Empirical Study of Industry and Firm Effects in the Biopharmaceutical Industry." *Research Policy* 30, pp. 1235–51.

Rothaermel, F.T. 2002. "Technological Discontinuities and Interfirm Cooperation: What Determines a Start-Up's Attractiveness as Alliance Partner?" *IEEE Transactions on Engineering Management* 49, no. 4, pp. 57–68.

Rothaermel, F.T., and C.W. Hill. 2005. "Technological Discontinuities and Complementary Assets: A Longitudinal Study of Industry and Firm Performance." *Organization Science* 16, no. 1, pp. 52–70.

Rothman, H., and H. Kraft. 2006. "Downstream and Into Deep Biology: Evolving Business Models in 'Top Tier' Genomics Companies." *Journal of Commercial Biotechnology* 12, no. 2, pp. 86–98.

Rust, R.T., and M. Huang. 2012. "Optimizing Service Productivity." *Journal of Marketing* 76, no. 2, pp. 47–66.

Sandström, C., M. Magnusson, and J. Jörnmark. 2009. "Exploring Factors Influencing Incumbents' Response to Disruptive Innovation." *Creativity and Innovation Management* 18, no. 1, pp. 8–15.

Sarasvathy, S.D. 2001. "Causation and Effectuation: Toward a Theoretical Shift from Economic Inevitability to Entrepreneurial Contingency." *Academy of Management Review* 26, no. 2, pp. 243–263.

Sashkin, M., and W.E. Rosenbach. 1998. "A New Vision of Leadership." In *Contemporary issues in leadership,* eds. W.E. Rosebach and R.L. Taylor, 4th ed. Boulder Colorado: Westview Press.

Savory, C, 2006. "Translating Knowledge to Build Technological Competence." *Management Decision* 44, no. 8, pp. 1052–75.

Schaer, M. 2015. "Watch Out for Dyson." *Fast Company,* pp. 126–143.

Schoen, J., T.W. Mason, W.A. Kline, and R.M. Bunch. 2005. "The Innovation Cycle: A New Model and Case Study for the Invention to Innovation Process." *Engineering Management Journal* 17, no. 3, pp. 3–10.

Schreyogg, G., and M. Kliesch-Eberl. 2007. "How Dynamic Can Organizational Capabilities Be? Towards a Dual-Process Model of Capability Dynamization." *Strategic Management Journal* 28, no. 9, pp. 913–933.

Schumpeter, J.A. 1934. *The Theory of Economic Development.* Boston, MA: Harvard University Press.

Schumpeter, J.A. 1954. *History of Economic Analysis.* Oxford, UK: Oxford University Press.

Sen, A. 2010. "Developing Ambidextrous, Connected and Mindful Brains for Contemporary Leadership." *International Journal of Business Insights and Transformation* 3, no. 2, pp. 103–111.

Shane, S. 2000. "Prior Knowledge and the Discovery of Entrepreneurial Opportunities." *Organization Science* 11, no. 4, pp. 448–469.

Shane, S. 2003. *A General Theory of Entrepreneurship: The Individual-Opportunity Nexus.* Cheltenham, U.K: Edward Elgar.

Sharma, A. 1999. "Central Dilemmas of Managing Innovation in Large Firms." *California Management Review* 41, no. 3, pp. 1–18.

Shen, X. 2010. "Understanding the Evolution of Rice Technology in China— From Traditional Agriculture to GM Rice Today." *Journal of Development Studies* 46, no. 6, pp. 1026–46.

Shi, M., J. Chiang, and B. Rhee. 2006. "Price Competition with Reduced Consumer Switching Costs: The Case of 'Wireless Number Portability' in the Cellular Phone Industry." *Management Science* 52, no. 1, pp. 27–38.

Shimizu, H. 2010. "Different Evolutionary Paths: Technological Development of Laser Diodes in the US and Japan 1960–2000." *Business History* 52, no. 7, pp. 1151–81.

Shostak, S. 2005. "The Emergence of Toxicogenomics: A Case Study of Molecularization." *Social Studies of Science* 35, no. 3, pp. 367–403.

Sierzchula, W., S. Bakker, K. Maat, and B. van Wee. 2015. "Alliance Formation in the Automobile Sector During an Era of Ferment." *Creativity and Innovation Management* 24, no. 1, pp. 109–121.

Simard, C., and J. West. 2006. "Knowledge Networks and the Geographic Locus of Innovation." In *Open innovation: Researching a new paradigm,* eds.

H. Chesbrough, W. Vanhaverbeke, and J. West, 222–240. Oxford, UK: Oxford University Press.

Simsek, Z., C. Heavey, J.F. Veiga, and D. Souder. 2009. "A Typology for Aligning Organizational Ambidexterity's Conceptualizations, Antecedents, and Outcomes." *Journal of Management Studies* 46, no. 5, pp. 864–94.

Szulanski, G. 1996. "Exploring Internal Stickiness: Impediments to the Transfer or Knowledge Within Firms." *Strategic Management Journal* 17, no. S2, pp. 27–43.

Smith, K. 2009. "Umbilical Cord Blood Banks: Modern Day Alchemy." *Journal of Commercial Biotechnology* 15, no. 3, pp. 236–244.

Smith, K.G., C.J. Collins, and K.D. Clark. 2005. "Existing Knowledge, Knowledge Creation Capability, and the Rate of New Product Introduction in High-Technology Firms." *Academy of Management Journal* 48, pp. 346–357.

Smith, R. 2010. "Google Means Everything." *Research Technology Management* 53, no. 1, pp. 67–69.

Smith, S., T. Ward, and J.S. Schumacher. 1993. "Constraining Effects of Examples in a Creative Generation Task." *Memory and Cognition* 21, no. 6, pp. 837–845.

Song, M., S. Im, H.V.D. Bij, and L.Z. Song. 2011. "Does Strategic Planning Enhance or Impede Innovation and Firm Performance?" *Journal of Product Innovation Management* 28, no. 4, pp. 503–520.

Srivastava, S.C., and G. Shainesh. 2015. "Bridging the Service Delivery Divide Through Digitally Enabled Service Innovation: Evidence from Indian Healthcare Service Providers." *MIS Quarterly* 39, no. 1, pp. 245–267.

Steele, R., K. Min, and A. Lo. 2012. "Personal Health Records Architecture." *Journal of American Society for Information Sciences* 63, no. 6, pp. 1079–91.

Steers, R.M., C.J. Sanchez-Runde, and L. Nardon. 2012. "Culture, Cognition, and Managerial Leadership." *Asia Pacific Business Review* 18, no. 3, pp. 425–439.

Sternberg, R., and T. Lubart. 1999. "The Concept of Creativity: Prospects and Paradigms." In *Handbook of creativity,* ed. R. Sternberg, 34–46. New York, NY: Cambridge University Press.

Stoker, J.I., J.C. Looise, O.A. Fisscher, and R.D. de Jong. 2001. "Leadership and Innovation: Relations Between Leadership, Individual Characteristics and the Functioning of R&D Teams." *International Journal of Human Resource Management* 12, no. 7, pp. 1141–51.

Stringham, E., J. Miller, and J.R. Clark. 2015. "Overcoming Barriers to Entry in an Established Industry: Tesla Motors." *California Management Review* 57, no. 4, pp. 85–103.

Styhre, A. 2011. "Competing Institutional Logics in the Biopharmaceutical Industry." *Creativity and Innovation Management* 20, no. 4, pp. 311–319.

Sviokla, T.T., and R.P. Shapiro. 1993. *Keeping customers*. Cambridge, MA: Harvard Business Press.

Swiercz, P.M., and S.R. Lydon. 2002. "Entrepreneurial Leadership in High-tech Firms: A Field Study." *Leadership and Organizational Development Journal* 23, no. 7, pp. 380–89.

Teece, D.J. 2007. "Explicating Dynamic Capabilities: The Nature and Microfoundations of Sustainable Enterprise Performance." *Strategic Management Journal* 28, no. 3, pp. 1307–22.

Teece, D.J. 2009. *Dynamic Capabilities and Strategic Management: Organizing for Innovation and Growth*. Oxford, UK: Oxford University Press.

Teece, D.J., G. Pisano, and A. Shuen. 1997. "Dynamic Capabilities and Strategic Management." *Strategic Management Journal* 18, no. 7, pp. 509–533.

Tell, J. 2000. "Learning Networks—A Metaphor for Inter Organizational Development in SMEs." *Enterprise and Innovation Management Studies* 1, no. 3, pp. 303–317.

Thacker, E. 2006. *The Global Genome: Biotechnology, Politics and Culture*. Cambridge, MA: MIT Press.

Thamhain, H.J. 2003. "Managing Innovative R&D Teams." *R&D Management* 33, no. 3, pp. 297–312.

Titus, R., and D. Sengupta. 2011. "Custom-Standardization'—Uncovering the Basis for Global Chaining Strategy in Prepared Food Retail." *Journal of Business and Retail Management Research* 6, no. 1, pp. 39–47.

Townsend, J., and R. Calantone. 2014. "Evolution and Transformation of Innovation in the Global Automotive Industry." *Journal of Product Innovation Management* 31, no. 1, pp. 4–7.

United Nations. 2003. Water for People, Water for Life-The United Nations World Water Development Report. Paris: UNESCO Publishing.

Uotila, T., and T. Ahlqvist. 2008. "Linking Technology Foresight and Regional Innovation Activities: Network Facilitating Innovation Policy in Lahti Region, Finland." *European Planning Studies* 16, no. 10, pp. 1423–43.

Van den Bergh, R. 2016. "Vertical Restraints: The European Part of the Policy Failure." *Antitrust Bulletin* 61, no. 1, pp. 167–185.

Vandervert, L. 2011. "How Thomas Edison Used a Results Focus to Produce Constant Invention and Innovation." *Board Leadership* 11, no. 7, pp. 1–8.

Varga, L., and P.M. Allen. 2006. "A Case-Study of the Three Largest Aerospace Manufacturing Organizations: An Exploration of Organizational Strategy, Innovation and Evolution." *Complexity and Organization* 8, no. 2, pp. 48–64.

Von Hippel, E. 1994. "Sticky Information and the Locus of Problems: Implications for Innovation." *Management Science* 40, no. 4, pp. 429–439.

Von Hippel, E. 1998. "Economics of Product Development by Users: the Impact of 'sticky' Local Information." *Management Science* 44, no. 5, pp. 629–644.

Wada, K., and T. Shibata. 2007. "Living with Robots; Its Socio-Psychological and Physiological Influences on the Elderly at a Care House." *IEEE Transactions on Robotics* 23, no. 5, pp. 972–980.

Watanabe, K., and B.W. Ane. 2003. "Coevolution of Manufacturing and Service Industry Functions." *Journal of Services Research* 3, no. 1, pp. 32–43.

Watson T.J., Jr., and P. Petre. 1990. *Father, Son & Co: My Life at IBM and Beyond.* London: Bantam Books.

Werner, T. 2010. "Next Generation Sequencing in Functional Genomics." *Briefings in Bioinformatics* 11, no. 5, pp. 499–511.

Wheelwright, S.C., and K. Clark. 1992. "Creating Project Plans to Focus Product Development." *Harvard Business Review*, pp. 1–14.

Whittington, R. 2003. "The Work of Strategizing and Organizing: A Practice Perspective." *Strategic Organization* 1, no. 1, pp. 117–126.

Williams, J. 2012. "The Value of Mobile Apps in Health Care." *Healthcare Financial Management* 66, no. 6, pp. 96–103.

Williamson, M. 2014. "Here be the Dragon: The Rise of SpaceX and the Journey to Mars." *Engineering and Technology* 9, no. 9, pp. 97–98.

Withers, M.C., P.L. Drnevich and L. Marino. 2011. "Doing More with Less: The Disordinal Implications of Firm Age for Leveraging Capabilities for Innovation Activity." *Journal of Small Business Management* 49, no. 4, pp. 515–36.

Witt, U. 1998. "Firms as Realizations of Entrepreneurial Visions." *Journal of Management Studies* 44, no. 7, pp. 1126–32.

Winter, S.G. 2003. "Mistaken Perceptions: Cases and Consequences." *British Journal of Management* 14, no. 1, pp. 39–44.

Wright, A. 2012. "The Social Life of Robots." *Communications of the ACM* 55, no. 2, pp. 41–49.

Wright, C.S., and I. Dawood. 2009. "Information Technology: Market Success to Succession." *The Review of Business Information Systems* 13, no. 4, pp. 7–20.

Zahra, S.A., and W.C. Bogner. 1999. "Technology Strategy and Software New Ventures' Performance: Exploring the Moderating Effect of the Competitive Environment." *Journal of Business Venturing* 15, pp. 135–173.

Zahra, S.A., and G. George. 2002. "Absorptive Capacity: A Review, Reconceptualization, and Extension." *Academy of Management Review* 27, no. 2, pp. 185–203.

Zeithmal, V.A., and M.J. Bitner. 1996. *Services Marketing.* New York, NY: McGraw Hill.

Zhenga, W., A.E. Khoury, and C. Grobmeiera. 2010. "How Do Leadership and Context Matter in R&D Team Innovation?—A Multiple case Study." *Human Resource Development International* 13, no. 3, pp. 265–83.

Index

www.ingramcontent.com/pod-product-compliance
Lightning Source LLC
Chambersburg PA
CBHW060548210326
41519CB00014B/3395